Contents

INTRODUCTION

Welcome to 'Cocotte Cuisine: 104 Delicious Recipes', the perfect cookbook for everyone who loves a good home-cooked meal. This cookbook is full of flavorful and delicious recipes that will have you cooking like a pro in no time. Our recipes are professional, yet accessible to the home cook. Whether you are an experienced cook looking for new recipes to add to your repertoire, a beginner cook just getting started, or someone who just wants to try their hand at making something new, this cookbook has something for everyone.

The recipes in 'Cocotte Cuisine' are heavily influenced by French cooking traditions, and feature classic dishes like Coq au Vin, Confit de Canard, and Tarte Tatin. We include recipes from all the major French regions, so you can experience the authentic flavors of the French countryside in your kitchen. We also have included some "fusion" recipes which combines traditional French flavors with those of other culinary cultures, like Moroccan Tagine and Persian-Inspired Couscous.

In addition to featuring classic French dishes, 'Cocotte Cuisine' also includes recipes for more straightforward dishes like Burgers with Brie and Rustic Vegetable Tart. We want to make sure that there is something for everyone, no matter their cooking level or dietary restrictions. The recipes in this cookbook are all quick and easy to make, with minimal prep time. We believe in cooking good food without all the fuss.

We want to help make cooking at home a enjoyable and rewarding experience. With this cookbook in hand you can spend more quality time sharing meals with your family and friends and less time worrying about lengthy recipes. If you're looking to master French cooking, an all-inclusive cookbook like 'Cocotte Cuisine' is the perfect place to start. We've taken the guesswork out of cooking and made sure that every recipe is clear and simple enough for anyone to follow. So pick up a pot and get cooking— you're in for a treat!

1. Coq au Vin

Coq au vin is a French classic dish that is well-loved for its unique blend of flavors and complexity. Chicken is slowly braised in red wine, veggies, and herbs, resulting in a flavorful and comforting dish.
Serving: 4-6
Preparation Time: 25 minutes
Ready Time: 1½-2 hours

Ingredients:
- 1 tablespoon olive oil
- 1 large yellow onion, chopped
- 2 cloves garlic, minced
- 1 teaspoon fresh thyme leaves
- 6 boneless, skinless chicken thighs
- Kosher salt, to taste
- Freshly ground black pepper
- ¼ cup cognac or brandy
- 2 cups low-sodium chicken broth
- 2 cups dry red wine
- 2 tablespoons tomato paste
- 8 ounces baby bella mushrooms, halved
- ½ cup frozen pearl onions
- 2 tablespoons unsalted butter
- 2 tablespoons freshly chopped parsley leaves

Instructions:
1. Heat the oil in a large Dutch oven or other heavy-bottomed pot over medium-high heat.
2. Add the onion and cook, stirring occasionally, until softened, 4-5 minutes
3. Add the garlic and thyme and cook until fragrant, about 1 minute.
4. Add the chicken and season with salt and pepper. Cook, stirring occasionally, until golden brown, about 5 minutes.
5. Deglaze the pot with the cognac or brandy, scraping up any browned bits from the bottom.
6. Add the chicken broth, wine, tomato paste, mushrooms and pearl onions, and bring to a simmer.

7. Reduce the heat to medium-low and simmer, stirring occasionally, until the chicken is cooked through and the sauce is thickened, 1-1½ hours.

8. Stir in the butter and parsley and season with additional salt and pepper, if desired.

Nutrition information:
Calories: 577
Total Fat: 24.3g
Carbohydrates: 16.5g
Protein: 57.3g

2. Beef Bourguignon

Beef Bourguignon is a classic French dish of beef braised in red wine, flavored with garlic, mushrooms and bacon. It is hearty, flavorful and perfect for a dinner party or special occasion.
Serving: 6
Preparation time: 15 minutes
Ready time: 3 hours

Ingredients:
• 2 1/2 pounds of boneless beef chuck, cut into 2-inch cubes
• 5 slices of bacon, diced
• 1 onion, chopped
• 4 cloves of garlic, minced
• 4 ounces of mushrooms, sliced
• 2 tablespoons of tomato paste
• 2 tablespoons of all-purpose flour
• 2 cups of dry red wine
• 3 cups of beef broth
• 2 bay leaves
• 1 teaspoon of dried thyme
• Salt and pepper, to taste
• 2 tablespoons of butter
• 2 tablespoons of chopped parsley

Instructions:

1. Season the beef cubes with salt and pepper. Heat 2 tablespoons of oil in a large pot over medium-high heat, and add the beef cubes in batches and brown on all sides. Transfer to a plate and set aside.

2. Reduce the heat to medium, add the bacon to the pot and cook until crispy. Add the chopped onion and garlic, and cook for 3 to 4 minutes, until softened. Add the mushrooms and cook for an additional 3 to 4 minutes.

3. Add the tomato paste and flour to the pot, stirring to coat the vegetables. Pour in the wine and beef broth, stirring to combine. Add the bay leaves and thyme, and season with additional salt and pepper, to taste.

4. Return the beef to the pot, and bring to a boil. Reduce the heat to low and simmer, covered, for 2 to 3 hours, stirring occasionally, until the beef is tender.

5. Remove from the heat, stir in the butter and parsley, and adjust the seasoning. Serve warm.

Nutrition information (per serving):
Calories: 490
Carbs: 8g
Protein: 36g
Fat: 24
Sodium: 470mg

3. Ratatouille

Ratatouille is a traditional French stewed vegetable dish that is full of flavour and nutrition. It is made with a variety of vegetables including tomatoes, eggplant, zucchini, bell peppers, and onions, and seasoned with herbs and spices.
Serving: 6
Preparation Time: 20 minutes
Ready Time: 1 hour

Ingredients:
• 2 tablespoons olive oil
• 1 onion, chopped
• 2 garlic cloves, minced

- 2 bell peppers, chopped
- 1 zucchini, diced
- 1 eggplant, diced
- 2 cups diced tomatoes
- 2 tablespoons chopped fresh basil
- 2 tablespoons chopped fresh oregano
- Salt and pepper to taste

Instructions:
1. Heat the olive oil in a large pot over medium heat.
2. Add the onion and garlic and sauté until softened, about 5 minutes.
3. Add the bell peppers, zucchini, eggplant, and tomatoes and cook for 10 minutes.
4. Add the basil, oregano, salt, and pepper and simmer for 15 minutes.
5. Serve warm.

Nutrition information: Per serving (1/6 of recipe): 181 calories, 11.2 g fat, 0.8 g saturated fat, 13.3 g carbohydrates, 6 g protein, 4.3 g fiber, 447 mg sodium.

4. Bouillabaisse

Bouillabaisse is a classic French seafood stew from the port city of Marseilles. It typically contains fish and other seafood cooked in a flavorful broth.
Serving: 8
Preparation time: 25 minutes
Ready time: 1-1/2 hours

Ingredients:
- 2 tablespoons of olive oil
- 1 onion, diced
- 2 cloves garlic, minced
- 2 stalks celery, diced
- 1 large carrot, diced
- 1 fennel bulb, diced
- 1 teaspoon paprika
- 1 teaspoon saffron

- 2 bay leaves
- 6 cups vegetable or chicken stock
- 8 ounces white fish (cod, halibut, or tilapia)
- 8 ounces salmon
- 12 ounces mussels
- 8 ounces shrimp
- 2 tablespoons fresh parsley, chopped

Instructions:
1. Heat the olive oil in a large soup pot over medium heat.
2. Add the onion, garlic, celery, carrot, and fennel, and cook until the vegetables are softened, about 5 minutes.
3. Add the paprika, saffron, bay leaves, and stock, and bring to a boil. Reduce the heat and simmer for 30 minutes.
4. Add the fish, salmon, mussels, and shrimp to the pot and simmer for 10 minutes, or until the fish is cooked through.
5. Remove from the heat and stir in the parsley.
6. Serve the bouillabaisse with crusty bread.

Nutrition information: (Per Serving)
- Calories: 350
- Total Fat: 10g
- Saturated Fat: 1.5g
- Cholesterol: 150mg
- Sodium: 440mg
- Carbohydrates: 13g
- Fiber: 3g
- Protein: 31g

5. Cassoulet

Cassoulet is a traditional French stew made with beans, pork, poultry, and sausage. The Ingredients are slowly cooked together to create a rich, deeply flavorful, and incredibly comforting dish. It's a great dish to make and enjoy for any occasion.
Serving: Serves 10-12.
Preparation Time: 20 minutes.
Ready Time: 1 hour, 30 minutes.

Ingredients:
- 2 lbs dried white beans (such as cannelini or Great Northern)
- 2 onions, diced
- 4 cloves garlic, minced
- 2 tsp dried thyme
- 1 bay leaf
- 12 oz smoked bacon, roughly chopped
- 1 lb smoked sausage, cut into bite-sized pieces
- 1 rotisserie chicken, shredded
- 2 cups chicken broth
- 1 cup white wine
- 1 tsp freshly ground black pepper
- 1 tsp salt
- 1 cup breadcrumbs

Instructions:
1. Soak the beans in water for 8 hours – it's best to soak them overnight.
2. Preheat the oven to 350°F.
3. In a large Dutch oven, heat the bacon over medium heat and cook until the fat has rendered, about 8 minutes.
4. Add the onions, garlic, thyme, and bay leaf and cook until the onions are soft, about 5 minutes.
5. Add the sausage and cook until lightly browned, about 5 minutes.
6. Add the chicken and cook until heated through, about 5 minutes.
7. Add the beans, chicken broth, wine, black pepper, and salt. Stir to combine.
8. Cover the Dutch oven and place in the preheated oven. Bake for 1 hour, stirring at least once during cooking time.
9. Remove from the oven and stir in the breadcrumbs.
10. Return to the oven and continue baking, uncovered for 30 minutes more.

Nutrition information: Per serving, Calories 300, Protein 24 g, Total Fat 10 g, Sat Fat 4 g, Total Carbohydrate 30 g, Dietary Fiber 9 g, Sugar 2 g, Sodium 644 mg.

6. Chicken Fricassee

Chicken Fricassee is an old-fashioned classic French dish made with chicken, mushrooms, and vegetables cooked in a thick creamy sauce. It's easy to make with simple Ingredients, yet has an elegant, flavorful taste.
Serving: Serves 4
Preparation Time: 15 mins
Ready Time: 1 hr

Ingredients:
- 2 pounds chicken legs and thighs
- 2 tablespoons olive oil
- 1 large onion, diced
- 1 clove garlic, minced
- 2 tablespoons flour
- 2 cups chicken broth
- 1 cup white wine
- 2 tablespoons fresh parsley, chopped
- 1 teaspoon fresh thyme leaves
- 8 ounces mushrooms, sliced
- 2 carrots, sliced
- 2 tablespoons butter
- 2 tablespoons heavy cream
- Salt and pepper to taste

Instructions:
1. Preheat oven to 350 degrees F.
2. In a large skillet heat olive oil over medium heat.
3. Add chicken pieces and cook until browned, about 8 minutes. Remove chicken to a plate and set aside.
4. Add onion to the pan and cook until softened, about 5 minutes. Add garlic and cook for 1 minute.
5. Add flour and stir to combine. Cook for 1 minute.
6. Add broth, wine, parsley and thyme and bring to a simmer.
7. Add mushrooms and carrots and simmer for 8 minutes.
8. Return chicken to the pan, cover and place in the preheated oven.
9. Bake for 30 minutes.
10. Remove pan from oven and stir in butter and cream.
11. Season with salt and pepper to taste.
12. Serve hot with cooked rice or mashed potatoes.

Nutrition information:
Calories: 288, Fat: 12 g, Carbohydrates: 9 g, Protein: 29 g, Cholesterol: 90 mg, Sodium: 308 mg, Fiber: 1 g, Sugar: 3 g

7. Duck Confit

Duck Confit is a classic French dish, consisting of a slow-cooked duck leg that has been salted and cooked in its own fat. The rich and succulent meat is tender and flavorful, and perfect served as part of a larger meal.
Serving: 4
Preparation Time: 9 hours
Ready Time: 9 hours

Ingredients:
• 4 duck legs
• 2 tablespoons of sea salt
• 2 tablespoons of freshly ground black pepper
• 2 tablespoons of smoked paprika
• 2 sprigs of thyme
• 2 bay leaves
• 2 tablespoons of garlic powder
• 2 tablespoons of ground allspice
• 2 quarts of duck fat

Instructions:
1. Rub the duck legs with salt, black pepper, smoked paprika, thyme, bay leaves, garlic powder, and allspice.
2. Place the legs in a dish, cover with cling film, and refrigerate for 8 hours.
3. Preheat oven to 225 degrees Fahrenheit.
4. Place the duck legs in an oven-safe dish and pour duck fat over them.
5. Cover the dish with aluminium foil and bake for 3 hours, or until the legs are very soft.
6. Turn the oven to the broiling setting and remove the foil.
7. Broil the duck legs for 10 minutes, or until the skin is crisp and golden.
8. Remove from the oven and let cool for 10 minutes before serving.
Nutrition Info:

Per Serving:
Calories - 545
Fat - 42g
Protein - 36g
Carbohydrates - 2g
Sugar - 0g

8. Escargots de Bourgogne

Escargots de Bourgogne is a classic French recipe of snails simmered in a delicious garlic-parsley butter. It's a simple yet impressive dish that can be served as an appetizer or as a main course.
Serving
Serves 4
Preparation time: 15 minutes
Ready time: 30 minutes

Ingredients:
• 24 snails (escargots)
• 2 tablespoons butter
• 2 tablespoons olive oil
• 2 cloves garlic, finely minced
• 5 tablespoons parsley, finely minced
• Salt and pepper, to taste

Instructions:
1. Rinse snails under cold running water, drain and dry on paper towels.
2. In a large saute pan or skillet, heat the butter and olive oil together over medium heat until bubbly.
3. Add garlic, parsley, salt and pepper and saute for 1 minute.
4. Add the snails and saute for 3 minutes.
5. Reduce heat to low and cook for an additional 20 minutes, stirring occasionally.
6. Serve hot with toasted crusty bread.

Nutrition information
Per serving: 320 calories, 28g fat, 7g protein, 5g carbohydrate, 2g fiber

9. Beef Stew

Beef Stew is a classic, hearty dish packed with flavor and nutrition. It's a great meal for a chilly day and a family dinner.

Serving : 6

Preparation Time : 15 minutes

Ready Time : 2 hour

Ingredients:
- 2 tablespoons cooking oil
- 2 pounds cubed stew beef
- 1 teaspoon garlic powder
- 1 teaspoon garlic salt
- 1 teaspoon black pepper
- 3 tablespoons all-purpose flour
- 2 onions, diced
- 2 stalks of celery, chopped
- 4 carrots, chopped
- 2 potatoes, peeled and cubed
- 2 cups beef broth or stock
- 2 bay leaves
- 2 tablespoons Worcestershire sauce
- 2 tablespoons soy sauce
- 1 teaspoon dried thyme

Instructions:
1. Heat oil in a large pot over high heat. Add cubed beef and cook, stirring occasionally, until lightly browned. Add garlic powder, garlic salt and pepper.
2. Sprinkle flour over the beef and mix until beef is well coated.
3. Add onions, celery, carrots and potatoes. Stir everything together and cook for 5 minutes.
4. Pour in beef broth or stock, bay leaves, Worcestershire sauce and soy sauce. Bring to a boil and reduce to a low simmer.
5. Simmer for 1 1/2 hours or until beef is tender. Stir in dried thyme. Serve hot.

Nutrition information:

Calories : 375; Total Fat : 11.7 g; Cholesterol : 85 mg; Sodium : 1285 mg; Carbohydrates : 33.7 g; Protein : 37.6 g; Fiber : 6.1 g.

10. Boulangère Potatoes

Boulangère Potatoes is an French side dish made with potatoes, onions, and garlic. It is a classic comfort dish that is perfect for any occasion.
Serving: Makes 4-6 servings.
Preparation Time: 10 minutes
Ready Time: 50 minutes

Ingredients:
-3 pounds potatoes, sliced
-2 onions, chopped
-4 cloves garlic, minced
-4 tablespoons butter
-¼ teaspoon dried thyme
-2 cups beef or chicken broth
-Salt and pepper, to taste

Instructions:
1. Preheat the oven to 350°F (175°C).
2. Grease a 9x13-inch baking dish.
3. Layer potatoes, onions, and garlic in the baking dish.
4. Dot with butter and sprinkle with thyme.
5. Pour broth over the Ingredients and season with salt and pepper.
6. Cover the dish with a lid or aluminum foil.
7. Bake for 40 minutes.
8. Uncover and bake for an additional 10 minutes.
9. Serve hot.

Nutrition information: Per serving: 302 cal, 13 g fat, 5 g protein, 41 g carbs, 6 g fiber, 651 mg sodium.

11. Quiche Lorraine

Quiche Lorraine is a French tart made with bacon, Gruyere cheese and creamy custard.
Serving: 8
Preparation Time: 10min
Ready Time: 50min

Ingredients:
-3 slices bacon
-1 unbaked 9-inch deep dish pie shell
-1 small onion, minced
-1/2 cup shredded Swiss cheese
-2 tablespoons minced parsley
-3 eggs
-1 cup milk
-1/4 teaspoon salt
-Dash of cayenne pepper

Instructions:
1. Preheat oven to 375 degrees.
2. In a skillet, cook bacon until crisp; drain and crumble.
3. Spread evenly in pie shell; top with onion, cheese and parsley.
4. In a bowl, beat eggs, milk, salt and cayenne pepper; pour into shell.
5. Bake for 40 to 45 minutes, or until a knife inserted near center comes out clean. Let stand 10 minutes before cutting into wedges to serve.

Nutrition information: Calories: 320, Fat: 18g, Cholesterol: 91mg, Sodium: 373mg, Total Carbohydrates: 20g, Protein: 11g, Fiber: 1g

12. Gratin Dauphinois

Gratin Dauphinois is a classic French dish consisting of thinly sliced potatoes layered in a creamy sauce and then baked to perfection. It is flavourful, comforting and perfect for a special dinner or meal.
Serving: 4-6
Preparation time: 25 minutes
Ready time: 50 minutes

Ingredients:

- 3 pounds potatoes
- 1 ½ cups half and half
- 2 cloves garlic, minced
- ¼ cup grated Parmesan cheese
- 2 tablespoons olive oil
- 2 tablespoons chopped fresh parsley
- 1 teaspoon salt
- ½ teaspoon freshly ground black pepper

Instructions:
1. Preheat oven to 375°F.
2. Peel the potatoes and thinly slice them.
3. Heat olive oil in large skillet over medium heat. Add garlic and cook for about 2 minutes.
4. In a large bowl, combine potatoes, half and half, Parmesan cheese, parsley, salt and pepper. Mix well.
5. Spread potato mixture into a greased 9x13 baking dish.
6. Bake for 45 minutes, or until potatoes are tender and golden brown.

Nutrition information: Per serving (4): Calories 282, Total Fat 10.5 g, Saturated Fat 4.5 g, Cholesterol 17 mg, Sodium 1154 mg, Total Carbohydrate 37 g, Dietary Fiber 3 g, Protein 8 g

13. Tarte Tatin

Tarte Tatin is a famous French upside-down apple tart. It is typically made with thinly sliced apples laid into a buttered pan, a layer of caramel, and topped with puff pastry.
Serving: 8 servings
Preparation Time: 50 minutes
Ready Time: 1 hour 15 minutes

Ingredients:
- 7 medium apples
- 1/3 cup (74g) of sugar
- 4 tablespoons (56g) of butter
- Pinch of salt
- 1 sheet of puff pastry

Instructions:
1. Preheat oven to 350°F (177°C).
2. Peel, core, and slice the apples.
3. In a 9-inch cast iron skillet, melt the butter, add the apples, sugar, and salt, and cook over medium heat until the apples are softened and lightly browned – about 15 minutes.
4. Remove from heat and layer the sliced puff pastry over the apples, tucking it in around the edges of the skillet.
5. Bake in preheated oven for about 40 minutes, or until the pastry is golden brown.
6. Let cool for 10 minutes before inverting the tart onto a plate.

Nutrition information: per serving – 256 calories, 11.6g fat, 41.8g carbohydrates, 2g protein

14. Pissaladière

Pissaladière is a classic French favorite that features a sweet-and-salty flavor combo. This savory tart consists of a crisp-tender thin crust, topped with caramelized onions, anchovies, and olives.
Serving: Makes 8 servings
Preparation time: 20 minutes
Ready time: 40 minutes

Ingredients:
- 1 package ready-made pie crust
- 2 teaspoons olive oil
- 2 large onions, diced
- 1 tablespoon balsamic vinegar
- 2 cloves garlic, minced
- 2 tablespoons fresh parsley, finely chopped
- 5 anchovy fillets, finely chopped
- 1/4 cup black olives, pitted and coarsely chopped
- 1/4 teaspoon freshly ground pepper
- 4 ounces Gruyère cheese, grated

Instructions:

1. Preheat oven to 400°F. Unroll the pie crust and place it in a 9-inch tart pan. Crimp or flute the edges of the crust.
2. Heat the olive oil in a large skillet over medium heat. Add the onions and cook, stirring often, until lightly caramelized, about 10 minutes. Add the balsamic vinegar, garlic, parsley, anchovies, olives and pepper. Sauté for 3 minutes more.
3. Spread the onion mixture over the prepared crust. Sprinkle with the Gruyère cheese. Bake for 15 minutes, or until the edges of the crust are golden brown.

Nutrition information: Per serving: 259 calories, 16g fat (6g saturated fat), 24mg cholesterol, 327mg sodium, 18g carbohydrate (2g dietary fiber, 4g sugar), 8g protein.

15. Coquilles Saint-Jacques

Coquilles Saint-Jacques is a classic French dish made with the scallops' coral roe, butter, cream, and a touch of white wine. It is a rich and flavorful representation of French cuisine.
Serving: 4
Preparation time: 10 minutes
Ready time: 30 minutes

Ingredients:
- 4 scallops
- Coral roe
- 4 tablespoons butter
- 1/2 cup heavy cream
- 1/4 cup white wine
- Salt and pepper to taste

Instructions:
1. Preheat oven to 375 degrees F.
2. In a bowl, mix the coral roe, butter, cream, and white wine.
3. Add salt and pepper to the mixture, to taste.
4. Place the scallops in a baking dish and pour the mixture over them.
5. Bake in the preheated oven for 25-30 minutes.
6. Serve with a side dish of your choice.

Nutrition information:
Calories: 373, Fat: 32.4 grams, Carbs: 5.5 grams, Protein: 12.3 grams

16. Chicken Provençal

Chicken Provençal is a savory French dish made from chicken, fresh herbs, tomatoes, garlic and onion. It's a great main course for any meal and can be served alone or with a side of mashed potatoes or rice.
Serving: 4
Preparation time: 10 minutes
Ready time: 35 minutes

Ingredients:
- 4 skinless, boneless chicken breasts
- 2 tablespoons olive oil
- 3 cloves garlic, minced
- 1 small onion, chopped
- 2 red bell peppers, diced
- 1 teaspoon dried oregano
- 1 teaspoon dried thyme
- 1 teaspoon dried rosemary
- 2 cups diced tomatoes
- Salt and black pepper to taste

Instructions:
1. Preheat oven to 375 degrees F (190 degrees C).
2. Heat the olive oil in a large skillet over medium heat. Add the garlic, onion and bell peppers and cook until softened, about 5 minutes.
3. Place the chicken breasts into the skillet and season with oregano, thyme and rosemary. Cook until chicken is lightly browned, about 5 minutes per side.
4. Transfer the skillet with the chicken to the oven. Bake for 15 minutes, or until chicken is cooked through.
5. Remove the skillet from the oven and stir in the diced tomatoes. Return to the oven and bake for 5 more minutes.
6. Remove the skillet from the oven and serve the chicken Provençal with mashed potatoes or rice.

Nutrition information:
Per Serving: 363 calories; 16.7 g fat; 22.9 g carbohydrates; 33.2 g protein; 75 mg cholesterol; 815 mg sodium.

17. Moules Marinières

Moules Marinières is a classic French dish of mussels cooked in a sauce of white wine, butter, and shallots.
Serving: 4
Preparation Time: 10 minutes
Ready Time: 15 minutes

Ingredients:
• 2 pounds mussels, scrubbed and debearded
• 3 tablespoons unsalted butter
• 2 cloves garlic, minced
• 1 shallot, minced
• 1 cup dry white wine
• 2 tablespoons chopped parsley
• Salt and freshly ground black pepper

Instructions:
1. In a large pot over medium-high heat, melt butter.
2. Add the garlic, shallot, and a pinch each of salt and pepper. Cook until softened, about 3 minutes.
3. Add the wine and bring to a simmer.
4. Add the mussels, cover, and lower heat to medium.
5. Cook until the mussels open, about 5 minutes. Discard any mussels that do not open.
6. Remove the pot from heat and stir in chopped parsley.
7. Serve mussels in their cooking liquid with a crusty baguette.

Nutrition information: Serving size: ½ cup; Calories: 182; Fat: 9g; Saturated fat: 5.8g; Cholesterol: 48mg; Carbohydrates: 9.2g; Sugar: 0.9g; Protein: 12.2g; Sodium: 1144mg

18. Onion Soup

Onion Soup is a classic French dish which is both comforting and flavorful. It is made from a delectable combination of aromatic onions, broth, and herbs. Enjoy a bowl of savory onion soup with crusty bread for a satisfying meal.
Serving: 4
Preparation time: 10 minutes
Ready time: 30 minutes

Ingredients:
- 2 tablespoons of butter
- 4 large onions, chopped
- 8 cups of beef broth
- 3 cloves of garlic, minced
- 2 tablespoons of Worcestershire sauce
- 2 tablespoons of parsley, chopped
- Salt and pepper, to taste

Instructions:
1. Heat butter in a large pot over medium heat. Add the onion and sauté for 5 minutes.
2. Add beef broth, garlic, Worcestershire sauce, and parsley. Bring to a boil, reduce heat to low and simmer for 20 minutes.
3. Season with salt and pepper to taste.
4. Ladle the soup into 4 bowls and serve. Enjoy!

Nutrition information: (per serving)
Calories: 132 kcal
Fat: 6 g
Carbohydrates: 12 g
Protein: 7 g
Sodium: 1,370 mg

19. Croque Monsieur

Croque Monsieur is a classic French dish that is a savory combination of toast, Gruyere cheese, and ham.

Serving: 4
Preparation time: 10 minutes
Ready time: 15 minutes

Ingredients:
- 8 slices of white bread
- 4 slices of deli ham
- 4 ounces of Gruyere cheese, shredded
- 2 tablespoons of butter
- 2 tablespoons of all-purpose flour
- 2 cups of milk
- 1 tablespoon of Dijon mustard
- Salt and pepper to taste

Instructions:
1. Preheat oven to 375 degrees Fahrenheit.
2. Spread butter evenly on one side of each slice of bread.
3. Place 4 slices of bread, butter-side down, on a baking sheet.
4. Layer each slice of bread with a slice of ham, and top with the shredded Gruyere cheese.
5. Place the remaining slices of bread on the baking sheet, butter-side up.
6. Bake for 10 minutes, or until bread is golden brown and cheese has melted.
7. Meanwhile, make cheese sauce. In a saucepan, melt butter over medium heat. Whisk in flour until blended. Slowly whisk in milk and continue stirring until sauce thickens. Stir in Dijon mustard, and season with salt and pepper to taste.
8. Pour cheese sauce over Croque Monsieur.
9. Broil for 3-4 minutes until cheese sauce is bubbly and golden brown.
10. Serve warm.

Nutrition information: Calories: 332; Protein: 16g; Carbs: 33g; Fat: 14g; Cholesterol: 44mg; Sodium: 929mg; Fiber: 1g; Sugar: 9g.

20. Sole Meunière

Sole Meunière is a French classic dish of with browned butter and Lemon, usually served with boiled potatoes. This meal is easy to make yet incredibly delicious, perfect for a special occasion or just for lunch.

Serving: Sole Meunière typically serves two people.
Preparation time: It takes about 15 minutes to prepare this dish.
Ready time: It takes about 15 minutes to cook this meal.

Ingredients:
- 2 sole fillets
- 2 tablespoons butter
- 2 tablespoons flour
- 2 tablespoons freshly squeezed lemon juice
- Salt, to taste
- Pepper, to taste
- 2 tablespoons chopped fresh parsley, for garnish

Instructions:
1. Heat the butter in a large skillet over medium-high heat.
2. Dip the sole fillets in the flour and coat on both sides.
3. Add the floured fillets to the skillet and cook until golden brown on both sides, about 2 minutes per side.
4. Pour the lemon juice over the fish and season with salt and pepper.
5. Cook for an additional minute.
6. Serve the fish topped with the browned butter and garnished with parsley.

Nutrition information
Each serving of Sole Meunière provides 500 calories, 34g fat, 5g carbohydrates, 22g protein, and 250mg sodium.

21. Choucroute Garnie

Choucroute Garnie is a classic French dish of sauerkraut, potatoes, and sausages. It is hearty and satisfying, and the perfect comfort food to share with family and friends.
Serving: 6
Preparation Time: 5 minutes
Ready Time: 55 minutes

Ingredients:
- 2 tablespoons olive oil

- 2-3 leeks, washed & halved
- 2 garlic cloves, minced
- 2 pounds sauerkraut
- 1/2 cup dry white wine
- 2 tablespoons caraway seeds
- 1-2 tablespoons Dijon mustard
- 6 bratwursts
- 3 potatoes, cut into wedges
- Salt & freshly ground black pepper

Instructions:
1. Preheat oven to 375°F.
2. Heat olive oil in a large pot over medium-high heat. Add leeks and garlic and sauté for 3-4 minutes until softened.
3. Add sauerkraut, white wine, caraway seeds, and mustard and stir to combine.
4. Place bratwursts and potatoes on top of the sauerkraut. Sprinkle salt and pepper over the top.
5. Cover the pot with a lid and transfer to the oven. Bake for 40-45 minutes until the potatoes and bratwursts are cooked through.
6. Serve hot.

Nutrition information: Calories: 464, Fat: 22 g, Cholesterol: 71 mg, Sodium: 1661 mg, Carbs: 41 g, Fiber: 9 g, Sugars: 12 g, Protein: 22 g.

22. Steak Frites

Steak Frites, an incredible combination of steak and french fries, is a classic French meal. It makes for a delicious, satisfying entree that is sure to please.
Serving: 4 servings
Preparation Time: 20 minutes
Ready Time: 30 minutes

Ingredients:
- 2 lbs sirloin steak
- 2 tbsp olive oil

- 2-3 cloves garlic, minced
- 2 tsp fresh thyme, chopped
- Sea salt and freshly ground black pepper, to taste
- 2 lbs russet potatoes, peeled and cut into wedges
- 2-3 tbsp vegetable oil
- 2-3 tbsp fresh parsley, chopped

Instructions:
1. Preheat oven to 425°F (220°C).
2. In a medium bowl, combine olive oil, garlic, thyme, sea salt, and black pepper. Rub the steak with the mixture then place it on a baking sheet.
3. In a separate bowl, season the potato wedges with salt and pepper. Place them onto the baking sheet with the steak.
4. Bake in the preheated oven for 15-20 minutes, or until steak is cooked to desired doneness and potatoes are golden brown and crisp.
5. Transfer steak and potatoes to a platter and garnish with fresh parsley.

Nutrition information:
Calories: 443 kcal, Carbohydrates: 40 g, Protein: 33 g, Fat: 15 g, Sodium: 277 mg, Fiber: 4 g, Sugar: 1 g

23. Blanquette de Veau

Blanquette de Veau, also known as veal blanquette, is a classic French stew of tender veal, mushrooms, and carrots cooked in a simple white sauce.
Serving: Serves 4
Preparation time: 15 minutes
Ready time: 1 hour 10 minutes

Ingredients:
- 1-2 tablespoons vegetable oil
- 2 ½ pounds of veal shoulder or leg, cuth into 2-inch cubes
- 2 onions, peeled and finely chopped
- 2 cloves of garlic, finely chopped
- 12 ounces mushrooms, sliced
- 2 carrots, peeled and chopped
- 2 tablespoons tomato paste

- 2 tablespoons all-purpose flour
- 2 ¾ cups chicken or vegetable broth
- 2 tablespoons fresh chopped parsley
- 1 tablespoon unsalted butter
- Salt and pepper to taste

Instructions:
1. Heat the oil in a large pot over medium heat. Add the veal and cook for 5 minutes, stirring occasionally.
2. Add the onions and garlic and cook for another 3 minutes.
3. Add the mushrooms, carrots, tomato paste, and flour and stir to combine.
4. Add the broth and bring to a boil. Reduce the heat and simmer, covered, for 30 minutes.
5. Remove the lid and simmer for another 10 minutes.
6. Stir in the parsley and butter and season to taste with salt and pepper.
7. Serve hot.

Nutrition information: per serving: Calories 248, Total fat 12 g, Cholesterol 72 mg, Sodium 241 mg, Total carbohydrates 11 g, Dietary fiber 2 g, Sugars 4 g, Protein 21 g.

24. Pot-au-Feu

Pot-au-Feu is a traditional French dish consisting of a beef broth that is simmered with potatoes, carrots, leeks, and other vegetables.
Serving: 6
Preparation Time: 30 minutes
Ready Time: 6 hours

Ingredients:
-3-4 lbs beef
-2 onions
-1 leek
-2 celery
-2 carrots
-4 potatoes
-Thyme sprigs

-Bay leaves
-Salt & pepper

Instructions:
1. Start by seasoning the beef with salt and pepper.
2. Place beef in large Dutch oven or pot and add cold water to cover by 1inch.
3. Peel and quarter onions, cut the leek in half lengthwise and add the vegetables to the pot.
4. Add the herbs.
5. Bring to the boil over medium-high heat and simmer for 5 minutes.
6. Reduce the heat to low and simmer for 5-6 hours, or until the beef is tender.
7. Remove beef from the pot and strain the broth.
8. Add the potatoes and cook until tender.
9. Slice beef into thin slices and return to pot and serve.

Nutrition information:
Calories: 330 kcal
Protein: 27 grams
Fat: 13 grams
Carbohydrates: 22 grams
Fiber: 6 grams

25. Boeuf en Daube

Boeuf en Daube is a traditional French dish of beef braised in red wine with vegetables, herbs and spices. This hearty and flavorful stew will serve as a show-stopper for any dinner gathering.
Serving: 4-6
Preparation Time: 15 minutes
Ready Time: 2 hours 30 minutes

Ingredients:
• 2 ½ lbs beef chuck, cut into cubes
• ¼ cup red wine
• 2 large carrots, chopped
• 2 celery stalks, chopped

- 2 onions, chopped
- 3 cloves garlic, minced
- 2 bay leaves
- 2 sprigs fresh rosemary
- 1 sprig fresh thyme
- ½ teaspoon black peppercorns
- 1 teaspoon kosher salt
- 2 tablespoons extra virgin olive oil
- 2 cups beef stock

Instructions:
1. Heat the olive oil in a large Dutch oven over medium-high heat. When hot, add the beef cubes in batches and brown on all sides.
2. When all of the beef has been browned, return all of the beef cubes to the pot.
3. Add the carrots, celery, onions, garlic, bay leaves, rosemary, thyme, and peppercorns. Season with salt and stir everything together.
4. Pour in the red wine and beef stock, and stir again. Cover the pot with a lid and reduce heat to low.
5. Simmer for 2 hours or until beef is tender.
6. When done, remove the lid, increase heat to medium-high and reduce sauce for around 10 minutes.
7. Serve Boeuf en Daube with cooked egg noodles or mashed potatoes.

Nutrition information: Calories: 547; Fat: 32g; Saturated Fat: 10g; Cholesterol: 138mg; Carbohydrates: 11g; Fiber: 2g; Protein: 45g.

26. Salmon en Papillote

Salmon en Papillote is a dish that wraps the fish with staples like mushrooms and potatoes in parchment paper, making it a flavorful, healthy, and easy meal to prepare.
Serving: 2
Preparation Time: 10 minutes
Ready Time: 25 minutes

Ingredients:
- 2 salmon fillets

- 2 tablespoons olive oil
- Salt and pepper, to taste
- 2 cloves garlic, minced
- 2 tablespoons fresh parsley, chopped
- 2 tablespoons fresh dill, chopped
- ¼ cup mushrooms, sliced
- 1 medium potato, thinly sliced

Instructions:
1. Preheat oven to 400°F.
2. Place parchment paper onto a baking sheet.
3. Place salmon fillets skin side down onto parchment paper.
4. Drizzle olive oil on top of the salmon and season with salt and pepper.
5. Sprinkle garlic, parsley and dill onto the salmon.
6. Top the salmon with mushrooms and potatoes.
7. Fold the parchment paper over the salmon and crimp the edges.
8. Bake in the preheated oven for 25 minutes.
9. Carefully open the parchment paper and serve.

Nutrition information:
Calories: 602; Fat: 39.9 g; Saturated Fat: 6.5 g; Protein: 43.2 g; Cholesterol: 116 mg; Sodium: 335.5 mg; Carbohydrates: 15.9 g; Fiber: 2.5 g; Sugar: 1.4 g

27. Duck à l'Orange

Duck à l'Orange is a classic French dish consisting of roasted duck served with a sweet orange sauce. This dish is a great way to glamorize a special occasion dinner, as it takes a bit of extra time and is sure to impress.
Serving: Serves 4
Preparation time: 20 minutes
Ready time: 1 hour 20 minutes

Ingredients:
- 4 duck legs
- 1 tablespoon butter
- 2 oranges, juice and grated zest separated
- 2 tablespoons honey

- 2 tablespoons brown sugar
- 2 tablespoons Grand Marnier (optional)
- 2 tablespoons orange marmalade
- 2 tablespoons fresh thyme
- 1 teaspoon cornstarch
- Salt and pepper, to taste

Instructions:
1. Preheat oven to 400 F and set a rack in a roasting pan.
2. Rub the duck legs with butter and season with salt and pepper. Place in the roasting pan.
3. Roast the duck for 30 minutes.
4. Meanwhile, combine orange juice, honey, sugar, Grand Marnier, orange zest, orange marmalade, and thyme in a saucepan.
5. Simmer over low to medium heat until reduced by half.
6. In a small bowl, mix together cornstarch with 2 tablespoons of water.
7. Once the sauce has reduced, add the cornstarch to the sauce and whisk to combine.
8. Continue simmering on low heat until sauce thickens.
9. Once the duck is cooked through, glaze with the sauce and serve.

Nutrition information:
Calories: 282
Carbs: 19g
Fat: 14g
Protein: 18g
Sugar: 15g
Sodium: 170mg

28. Crème Brûlée

Crème Brûlée is a classic French dessert made of a creamy custard covered with a caramelized hard sugar shell. It's a rich and decadent dessert that is surprisingly simple to make.
Serving: 6
Preparation Time: 10 minutes
Ready Time: 2 hours

Ingredients:

- 3 large egg yolks
- 1/4 cup of sugar
- 2 cups of heavy cream
- 1 teaspoon of vanilla extract
- 1/4 cup of sugar for topping

Instructions:
1. Preheat oven to 325 degrees F (165 degrees C).
2. In a medium bowl, whisk together egg yolks and 1/4 cup of sugar until thick and creamy.
3. In a medium saucepan bring cream and vanilla to a simmer.
4. Gradually add the hot cream to the egg mixture, stirring constantly.
5. Pour the mixture into six (6-ounce) ramekins.
6. Place ramekins into a shallow baking pan.
7. Pour enough hot water into the baking pan to come halfway up the sides of the ramekins.
8. Bake for 45 minutes, or until crème brûlée is just set.
9. Remove ramekins from the baking pan and cool to room temperature.
10. Cover with plastic wrap and chill for at least 2 hours.
11. Preheat the oven broiler.
12. Sprinkle a layer of sugar over each custard.
13. Place ramekins on a baking sheet and place under the broiler until the sugar is golden-brown.

Nutrition information:
Calories: 400, Fat: 24g, Saturated Fat: 14g, Cholesterol: 131mg, Sodium: 44mg, Carbohydrates: 37g, Fiber: 0g, Sugar: 36g, Protein: 4g

29. Profiteroles

Profiteroles are delicious choux pastry puffs filled with sweet, creamy custard and covered in a smooth, rich chocolate sauce. Serve them with fresh fruit or cream for an indulgent party dish or dessert.
Serving: 8
Preparation Time: 45 minutes
Ready Time: 1 hour and 5 minutes

Ingredients:

-1 cup all-purpose flour
-1/4 teaspoon salt
-1/2 cup butter
-1 cup water
-4 large eggs
-1/2 teaspoon vanilla extract
-1 cup custard
-1 cup semi-sweet chocolate chips
-1/4 cup heavy cream

Instructions:
1. Preheat oven to 425 degrees F (220 degrees C). Line a baking sheet with parchment paper.
2. In a medium saucepan, bring the butter and water to a boil. Once boiling, remove from the heat and stir in the flour and salt until a smooth dough forms.
3. Add the eggs one at a time, stirring vigorously after each addition until everything is combined. Stir in the vanilla extract.
4. Drop the dough by spoonfuls onto the prepared baking sheet. Bake for 20-25 minutes until golden brown.
5. Once cooled, carefully make a slit in the side of each profiterole. Fill with custard.
6. In a small bowl, combine the chocolate chips and cream. Microwave until smooth and combined.
7. Dip the filled profiteroles in the chocolate glaze and let them cool.

Nutrition information: 254 calories, 14g fat, 28g carbohydrates, 3g protein

30. Confit de Canard

Confit de Canard is a French dish of duck cooked in its own fat. This traditional dish is flavorful and crispy and pairs great with a carbohydrate side like rice or potato.
Serving: 4-6 people
Preparation Time: 40 minutes
Ready Time: 4 hours

Ingredients:

-4 duck legs
-2 tablespoons of baking soda
-4 crushed garlic cloves
-2 tablespoons of coarsely ground pepper
-1-2 tablespoons of dried thyme or rosemary
-2 tablespoons of bay leaves
-2 tablespoons of coarse sea salt
-White pepper
-3 tablespoons of olive oil or duck fat

Instructions:

1. Preheat oven to 250°F.
2. Rinse duck legs and pat dry with paper towels.
3. In a shallow dish, combine baking soda, garlic, pepper, thyme or rosemary, bay leaves, salt, and white pepper.
4. Rub duck legs with the mixture and arrange in an oven-safe dish.
5. Drizzle olive oil or duck fat over the duck and massage it into the legs.
6. Cook in preheated oven for 3-4 hours until crisp and golden-brown.
7. Allow to cool before serving.

Nutrition information: Per Serving: 260 calories; 19.9 g fat; 7.6 g carbohydrates; 14.8 g protein.

31. Bouillabaisse Marseillaise

Bouillabaisse Marseillaise is a hearty and flavorful French fish stew that originated in the port city of Marseille. It has become an iconic dish of Provençal cuisine, featuring a blend of fresh fish, aromatic vegetables, and a flavorful broth.
Serving: 8
Preparation time: 45 minutes
Ready time: 1 hour 30 minutes

Ingredients:

- 2 pounds monkfish fillets
- 1 pound red mullet fillets
- 1 pound sea bass fillets

- 2 tablespoons olive oil
- 5 cloves garlic, minced
- 2 onions, minced
- 2 celery stalks, diced
- 2 carrots, diced
- 2 tablespoons tomato paste
- 1 teaspoon herbes de Provence
- 1 teaspoon saffron threads
- 1/2 teaspoon salt
- 2 bay leaves
- 4 cups vegetable broth
- 2 cups dry white wine
- 1/2 cup heavy cream
- 1/4 cup chopped fresh parsley

Instructions:
1. Preheat oven to 350 degrees Fahrenheit.
2. Place fish fillets on a baking sheet and season with salt and pepper. Bake for 15 minutes until cooked through.
3. Heat olive oil in a large Dutch oven over medium-high heat. Add garlic, onions, celery, and carrots, and cook until softened, about 5 minutes.
4. Add tomato paste, herbes de Provence, saffron, salt, and bay leaves. Stir to combine and cook for 1 minute.
5. Pour in vegetable broth and white wine. Bring to a boil and reduce heat to a simmer. Cover and cook for 25 minutes.
6. Add the cooked fish fillets to the Dutch oven and simmer for 10 minutes. Stir in cream and parsley.
7. Taste for seasoning and adjust if necessary. Serve immediately.

Nutrition information: Per serving: 447 calories; 32.5 g fat; 18 g carbohydrates; 22.5 g protein; 2.7 g fiber.

32. Soupe à l'Oignon

Soupe à l'Oignon is a traditional French soup made with caramelized onion and beef broth. It is a hearty and flavorful soup that will warm you up on a cold day.
Serving: 4

Preparation Time: 20 minutes
Ready Time: 1 hour

Ingredients:
- 4 tablespoons olive oil
- 6 medium onions, sliced
- 2 cloves garlic, minced
- 6 cups beef broth
- 1/2 cup dry white wine
- 2 tablespoons Worcestershire sauce
- 1 teaspoon dried thyme
- 1/2 teaspoon black pepper
- 3 tablespoons all-purpose flour
- 2 tablespoons cognac or brandy
- Salt to taste

Instructions:
1. Heat oil in a medium saucepan over medium heat. Add onions and garlic and cook until golden brown, stirring often, about 10 minutes.
2. Add beef broth, white wine, Worcestershire sauce, thyme and pepper. Stir to combine and bring to a boil. Reduce heat to low, cover and simmer for 30 minutes.
3. Dissolve flour in the cognac or brandy. Add to the soup and stir to combine. Simmer for 10 minutes more. Taste and adjust seasoning with salt, if desired.

Nutrition information (per serving): Calories: 330, Total Fat: 13 g, Cholesterol: 0 mg, Sodium: 434 mg, Total Carbohydrate: 21 g, Protein: 16 g

33. Salade Niçoise

Salade Niçoise is a classic French salad consisting of tomatoes, mixed greens, eggs, tuna, and black olives. It's perfect for a light lunch or a summer dinner.
Serving: Serves 4
Preparation Time: 10 minutes
Ready Time: 15 minutes

Ingredients:
- 4 tomatoes, sliced
- 2 cups mixed greens
- 2 hard-boiled eggs, sliced
- 1 can tuna, drained
- 10 pitted black olives
- 1/4 cup olive oil
- 2 tablespoons lemon juice
- 1 tablespoon dijon mustard
- salt and pepper to taste

Instructions:
1. In a large bowl, combine tomatoes, mixed greens, eggs, tuna, and olives.
2. In a separate bowl, whisk together olive oil, lemon juice, and dijon mustard.
3. Pour dressing over salad and mix.
4. Add salt and pepper to taste.

Nutrition information: Per serving (1/4 of salad): 140 calories, 11 g fat, 5 g carbohydrates, 4 g protein, 2 g fiber.

34. Pâté de Campagne

Pâté de Campagne is a coarsely-textured French pork-based country-style terrine or pâté, a form of large-size sausage.
Serving: 8
Preparation Time: 15 minutes
Ready Time: 3 to 4 hours

Ingredients:
• 1 trip pork shoulder, cut into ½-inch cubes
• 1 pound pork fatback, cut into ½-inch cubes
• 2 cloves garlic, peeled and minced
• 1 teaspoon fresh thyme leaves
• 1 teaspoon freshly ground black pepper
• 1 teaspoon kosher salt
• ⅛ teaspoon ground cloves
• 1 tablespoon brandy

• 1 teaspoon chopped fresh parsley

Instructions:
1. Preheat the oven to 350°F.
2. Place the cubed pork and fatback into a large mixing bowl.
3. Add the garlic, thyme, black pepper, salt, and cloves and toss to combine.
4. Add the brandy and parsley and mix until evenly distributed.
5. Grease a 2-quart terrine with oil or butter and line it with a double layer of parchment paper
6. Scoop the pork mixture into the terrine and spread it into an even layer.
7. Cover the terrine with a double layer of parchment paper and then cover with aluminum foil.
8. Place the terrine into a large shallow baking dish and then fill the dish with enough hot water to come halfway up the sides of the terrine.
9. Bake in the preheated oven for 1½ to 2 hours, or until the pork is cooked through.
10. Allow the pâté to cool completely before serving.

Nutrition information: Per serving: 310 calories; 23.3g fat; 6.6g carbohydrates; 15.3g protein; 65mg cholesterol; 369mg sodium.

35. Quenelles de Brochet

Quenelles de Brochet is a classic French dish made of pike-perch, which is poached, flaked, and blended with butter, cream and egg yolks before being shaped into light clouds of delicate goodness.
Serving: 4-6
Preparation Time: 30 minutes
Ready Time: 1 hour

Ingredients:
- 600g pike-perch fillets
- 2 tablespoons butter
- 4 tablespoons fresh cream
- 2 egg yolks
- Salt and pepper to taste

Instructions:
1. De-bone and skin the pike-perch fillets.
2. Break the fish into small pieces.
3. Put the pieces into a food processor and blend until smooth.
4. Melt the butter in a pan over low heat.
5. Add the fish mixture and stir.
6. Add the cream and egg yolks and stir until combined.
7. Cook for a few minutes until the mixture thickens.
8. Season with salt and pepper to taste.
9. Take the mixture off of the heat and allow to cool.
10. Once cooled, flake the fish again and shape into quenelles.
11. Put the quenelles into a greased baking tray and cook in a pre-heated oven at 180°C for about 30 minutes.

Nutrition information:
Calories: 340
Fat: 20g
Saturated Fat: 9g
Trans Fat: 0g
Carbohydrates: 1g
Protein: 35g
Cholesterol: 157mg
Sodium: 174mg

36. Grilled Ratatouille Tartines

Grilled Ratatouille Tartines is a scrumptious snack that combines crunchy crostini with a selection of healthy summer vegetables. It's easy to make and is an ideal recipe for a light lunch or picnic.
Serving: 4
Preparation Time: 20 minutes
Ready Time: 15 minutes

Ingredients:
- 4 crostini
- 2 tablespoons extra-virgin olive oil
- 1 onion, finely chopped

- 2 cloves of garlic, minced
- 1 eggplant, diced
- 1 red bell pepper, diced
- 1 yellow bell pepper, diced
- 1 zucchini, diced
- 2 sprigs of thyme
- 2 tablespoons chopped parsley
- 4 teaspoons of crumbled feta cheese
- Salt and pepper, to taste

Instructions:
1. Preheat the grill.
2. Brush the crostini with half of the extra-virgin olive oil.
3. Grill the crostini for 3-4 minutes each side until lightly golden and crisp.
4. Heat the remaining olive oil in a skillet over medium heat. Add the onion, garlic, eggplant, bell peppers, and zucchini. Sauté for 8-10 minutes until the vegetables are tender.
3. Add the thyme and season with salt and pepper.
4. Divide the ratatouille among the crostini and sprinkle with feta cheese.
5. Grill the tartines for 4-5 minutes until the cheese is melted.
6. Sprinkle with chopped parsley.
7. Serve the Grilled Ratatouille Tartines.

Nutrition information:
Calories: 201
Fat: 12 g
Total carbohydrate: 18 g
Dietary fiber: 5 g
Protein: 6 g

37. Brandade de Morue

Brandade de Morue is a traditional French dish made with salted cod, potatoes, garlic, lemon juice, olive oil, and cream. It's a creamy and flavorful dish that's perfect for cold winter nights.
Serving: 4-6
Preparation time: 10 minutes

Ready time: 40 minutes

Ingredients:
- 8 ounces salted cod, soaked overnight and shredded
- 2 pounds potatoes, peeled and cubed
- 5 cloves garlic, minced
- 2 tablespoons lemon juice
- 1/4 cup olive oil
- 1/2 cup heavy cream
- Salt and pepper to taste

Instructions:
1. Preheat the oven to 350 degrees F.
2. In a large pot, place the cubed potatoes in cold water with enough salt to just cover the potatoes. Bring to a boil over medium-high heat.
2. Once boiling, reduce heat to low and simmer for 15-20 minutes, until potatoes are fork tender.
3. Drain the potatoes, reserving ½ cup of the cooking liquid.
4. Transfer the potatoes to a large bowl. Add the shredded cod, minced garlic, lemon juice, olive oil, and cream. Mix until combined.
5. Grease the inside of a 9×13 inch baking dish with butter.
6. Transfer the potato mixture to the baking dish, spreading it evenly.
7. Cover with aluminum foil and bake for 35 minutes.
8. Remove foil and bake for an additional 5 minutes.
9. Remove from oven and let cool slightly before serving.

Nutrition information: Serving size – 1/6 of recipe. Calories – 218; Total fat – 10.3g; Saturated fat – 3.7 g; Cholesterol – 34mg; Sodium – 584mg; Total carbohydrate – 21.6g; Dietary fiber – 2.5 g; Protein – 8.9 g

38. Boudin Noir

Boudin Noir, also known as black pudding, is a traditional French pork sausage. It is made with an assortment of cooked pork parts, spices, onions, oats, and grains, resulting in a unique and savory flavor. The sausage is best enjoyed in a traditional recipe with apples, or in a variety of other dishes.

Serving: 6
Preparation Time: 15 minutes
Ready Time: 45 minutes

Ingredients:
-1 ½ lbs pork liver
-1 cup chopped onion
-1 garlic clove, minced
-1 cup rolled oats
-1 cup cooked barley
-½ teaspoon freshly ground black pepper
-1 teaspoon sea salt
-½ teaspoon ground cloves
-4 tablespoons chopped fresh parsley
-2 tablespoons snipped fresh chives
-3 tablespoons rapeseed (canola) oil

Instructions:
1. In a large bowl, combine the liver, onion, garlic and oats and mix until blended.
2. Add the barley, pepper, salt, cloves, parsley, and chives and mix until blended.
3. Divide the mixture into 6 equal portions.
4. Using waxed paper, into a log shape.
5 In a large skillet or Dutch oven, heat the oil over medium-high heat.
6. Add the boudin logs and cook for 10 minutes, turning every few minutes to brown them on all sides.
7. Reduce the heat to low and simmer for 30 minutes, turning once.

Nutrition information: Each serving contains 129 calories, 8.2g fat, 5.5g carbohydrates, and 7.8g protein.

39. Côte de Boeuf

Côte de Boeuf, or Beef Rib-eye Steak, is a delicious and flavorful cut of beef that is perfect for grilling or pan-frying.
Serving: 4
Preparation time: 10 minutes
Ready time: 15 minutes

Ingredients:
- 1 (2-inch thick) bone-in rib-eye steak, about 2 pounds
- 2 tablespoons olive oil
- 2 cloves garlic, minced
- 2 teaspoons fresh thyme leaves
- 2 teaspoons coarse sea salt
- 1 teaspoon freshly ground black pepper

Instructions:
1. Preheat a grill or grill pan to medium-high heat.
2. Rub the steak with the olive oil, garlic, thyme, salt, and pepper.
3. When the grill is hot, place the steak on the grill and cook for 4 minutes on each side, or to desired doneness.
4. Remove steak from the grill and let rest for 5 minutes before slicing.
5. Slice the steak against the grain and serve.

Nutrition information: 2 servings (4 ounces each) of Côte de Boeuf will provide approximately 400 calories, 25 grams of protein, 26 grams of fat, and 2 grams of carbohydrates.

40. Poulet Basquaise

Poulet Basquaise is a comforting and savory French dish comprised of chicken and vegetables simmered in a tomato-wine sauce.
Serving: 4
Preparation time: 25 minutes
Ready time: 55 minutes

Ingredients:
4 boneless, skinless chicken breasts
4 tablespoons olive oil
2 cloves garlic, minced
2 large onions, diced
2 red bell peppers, diced
2 green bell peppers, diced
1 (14.5 ounce) can diced tomatoes
1/2 cup white wine

1/4 teaspoon Espelette pepper or Cayenne pepper
Salt and ground black pepper, to taste

Instructions:
1. Heat the olive oil in a large skillet over medium heat.
2. Season the chicken breasts on both sides with salt and pepper, then add to the skillet and cook until lightly browned, about 5 minutes per side.
3. Add the garlic, onions, and peppers to the skillet and cook until the vegetables are soft, about 7 minutes.
4. Pour in the can of diced tomatoes and white wine, season with Espelette pepper or Cayenne pepper, and bring to a boil.
5. Reduce the heat to low and simmer until the chicken is cooked through, about 25 minutes.

Nutrition information: calories: 449, fat: 22g, saturated fat: 3g, cholesterol: 98mg, sodium: 248mg, carbohydrate: 23g, dietary fiber: 5g, sugar: 11g, protein: 32g

41. Pithiviers

Pithiviers is a classic French pastry filled with almond paste and topped with icing sugar, and is a popular dessert throughout France.
Serving: 8
Preparation time: 1 hour
Ready time: 1 hour and 20 minutes

Ingredients:
• 225g plain flour
• 125g butter
• 4tbsp iced water
• 225g almond paste
• Egg yolk
• Icing sugar for decoration

Instructions:
1. Put 225g plain flour into a bowl and rub in 125g butter until it has the consistency of fine breadcrumbs.

2. Stir in 4tbsp of iced water to form a dough, then wrap in cling film and chill in the fridge for 30 minutes.
3. Preheat the oven to 190°C/gas 5.
4. Roll the pastry out and use to line an 18cm round tart tin.
5. Fill with 225g of almond paste.
6. Brush the edges of the pastry with a beaten egg yolk.
7. Bake for 40 minutes or until golden brown.
8. Leave to cool for 10 minutes before decorating with icing sugar.

Nutrition information:
Calories: 574, Total fat: 32.2g; Saturated fat: 4.6g; Cholesterol: 72mg; Sodium: 29mg; Total carbohydrates: 54.8g; Dietary fiber: 3.5g; Sugars: 15.4g; Protein: 8.6g.

42. Petits Farcis

Petits Farcis are traditional stuffed vegetables from France, usually served as part of a starter or appetizer. They are a delicious way to make a vegetable dish stand out on your table.
Serving: 4
Preparation Time: 15 minutes
Ready Time: 40 minutes

Ingredients:
• 4 small vegetables, such as peppers, aubergines, and tomatoes
• 120g minced pork
• 120g minced beef
• 2 tablespoons of olive oil
• 2 garlic cloves, minced
• 1 teaspoon of smoked paprika
• 1 teaspoon of dried oregano
• 2 teaspoons of dried thyme
• Salt and pepper to taste
• 1 egg
• 2 tablespoons breadcrumbs

Instructions:
1. Preheat the oven to 180°C.

2. Cut each vegetable in half and hollow out the middle, leaving about a 1-centimetre border.
3. In a bowl, combine the minced pork and beef, olive oil, garlic, paprika, oregano, thyme, and salt and pepper to taste.
4. Place a spoonful of the mixture into each hollowed-out vegetable and press down gently.
5. In a small bowl, mix together the egg and breadcrumbs.
6. Brush this egg mixture over the tops and sides of each vegetable half.
7. Place the stuffed vegetables on a baking tray lined with parchment paper and cook in the oven for 30-40 minutes, or until the vegetables are cooked through and golden.

Nutrition information:
Calories: 276
Carbohydrates: 5 g
Fat: 14 g
Protein: 24 g
Sodium: 206 mg
Sugar: 2 g

43. Tarte Flambée

Tarte Flambee is a classic French pizza dish that is composed of a thin, crisp crust topped with creme fraiche, onions, bacon, and fresh herbs.
Serving: 4
Preparation time: 15 minutes
Ready time: 25 minutes

Ingredients:
- 6 ounces bacon, diced
- 1 large yellow onion, sliced
- 2 cloves garlic, minced
- 2 teaspoons chopped fresh thyme
- ½ teaspoon salt
- ¼ teaspoon freshly ground black pepper
- 1 teaspoon olive oil
- 8 ounces crème fraiche
- 2 (8-inch) round prepared pizza crusts

Instructions:
1. Preheat oven to 425 degrees Fahrenheit.
2. In a large skillet, cook bacon over medium heat for 8 minutes or until crisp. Remove bacon from pan and set aside.
3. In the same skillet, cook the onion, garlic, thyme, salt, and pepper in the oil over medium heat for 10 minutes or until the onion is softened and beginning to brown.
4. Spread a thin layer of the crème fraiche on each pizza crust. Sprinkle the bacon pieces over the top. Arrange the onion mixture over the bacon.
5. Place pizzas on a baking sheet. Bake for 15 minutes or until crust is lightly browned.

Nutrition information: Per serving: 250 calories, 14 g of fat, 4 g of saturated fat, 420 mg of sodium, 20 g of carbohydrates, 2 g of dietary fiber, 8 g of sugar, 11 g of protein.

44. Navarin d'Agneau

Navarin d'Agneau is a traditional French dish that is typically served as a main course. The dish is a stew of lamb and seasonal vegetables such as turnips, potatoes, carrots, and peas.
Serving: Serves 4-6
Preparation Time: 15 minutes
Ready Time: 40 minutes

Ingredients:
- 2 lb of diced lamb shoulder
- 2 tablespoons of olive oil
- 6-7 cloves of garlic, crushed
- 1 onion, diced
- 3-4 carrots, diced
- 2-3 tablespoons of tomato paste
- 3 cups of vegetable or chicken stock
- 2 cups of cubed potatoes
- 1 cup of turnip, cubed
- 1 cup of frozen peas
- Salt and freshly ground black pepper to taste

Instructions:
1. Heat the olive oil in a large pan over medium heat.
2. Add the garlic and onion and cook until the onion is translucent.
3. Add the lamb and stir to coat.
4. Add the carrots and cook for 5 minutes.
5. Add the tomato paste and mix well.
6. Add the stock and bring to a boil.
7. Reduce the heat to low and simmer for 30 minutes.
8. Add the potatoes, turnip, and peas and season with salt and pepper.
9. Simmer for an additional 10 minutes.
10. Serve hot.

Nutrition information: Calories 400; Total Fat 12g; Saturated Fat 3.5g; Sodium 240mg; Carbohydrates 29g; Sugars 6g; Protein 38g; Fiber 5g; Cholesterol 50mg.

45. Soupe de Poisson

Soupe de Poisson is a hearty seafood soup originating from France. It is a combination of white fish, garlic, onions, bitters, milk, and spices. It has a unique taste that is both savory and slightly sweet.
Serving: 6
Preparation Time: 15 minutes
Ready Time: 1 hour

Ingredients:
- 2 tablespoons olive oil
- 1 onion, chopped
- 2 cloves garlic, minced
- 1 teaspoon fresh thyme leaves
- 2 cups white fish fillets, cut into cubes
- 2 cups milk
- 2 cups chicken broth
- 2 tablespoons dry white wine
- 2 tablespoons bitters
- 1 bay leaf
- Salt and pepper, to taste

Instructions:

1. Heat the olive oil in a medium saucepan over medium-high heat.
2. Add the onion, garlic, and thyme and cook until the onion is softened, about 5 minutes.
3. Add the fish, milk, chicken broth, wine, bitters, and bay leaf. Bring the mixture to a boil.
4. Reduce the heat and simmer until the fish is cooked through, about 10 minutes.
5. Remove the bay leaf and season with salt and pepper.
6. Serve warm.

Nutrition information: Approximately 200 calories per serving, 6g of fat, 16g of protein, and 8g of carbohydrate.

46. Escargots à la Bourguignonne

Escargots à la Bourguignonne is a classic French dish that consists of snails cooked in a flavorful garlic and parsley butter sauce. This dish is known for its smooth and creamy texture, making it a delight to the taste-buds.
Serving: 4
Preparation time: 20 minutes
Ready time: 45 minutes

Ingredients:
- 2 lb. of canned snails
- 1 cup butter
- 3 cloves of garlic, minced
- 1/2 cup parsley, chopped
- 2 tbsp. of olive oil
- Salt and pepper, to taste

Instructions:
1. Preheat the oven to 375°F.
2. Heat the butter in a large skillet over medium heat and add the garlic and parsley. Cook for 2-3 minutes until the garlic is fragrant.
3. Add the snails to the pan with the butter and garlic mixture and stir until they are evenly coated.

4. Add the olive oil and season with salt and pepper to taste.
5. Transfer the snails and sauce to a baking dish and bake in the preheated oven for 30 minutes.
6. Serve hot.

Nutrition information: Calories: 400, Fat: 24g, Saturated Fat: 16g, Cholesterol: 40mg, Sodium: 410mg, Carbohydrates: 10g, Protein: 11g, Sugar: 2g

47. Poulet à la Moutarde

Poulet à la Moutarde is a classic French dish characterized by its smooth and creamy mustard sauce. This hearty meal is perfect for entertaining guests or a cozy evening at home.
Serving: 4
Preparation Time: 30 min
Ready Time: 1 hour

Ingredients:
- 4 chicken breasts
- 2 tablespoons of Dijon mustard
- 2 tablespoons of white wine
- 2 tablespoons of butter
- ½ cup of chicken broth
- 1 tablespoon of fresh parsley
- 1 teaspoon of fresh thyme
- Salt and pepper to taste

Instructions:
1. Preheat oven to 375°F.
2. Place chicken breasts in a baking dish.
3. In a separate bowl, mix together mustard, white wine, butter, chicken broth, parsley and thyme.
4. Spoon the mixture onto the chicken breasts, and season with salt and pepper to taste.
5. Bake in preheated oven for 30 minutes or until chicken is cooked through.
6. Serve and enjoy.

Nutrition information:
Calories: 265, Fat: 10 g, Protein: 32 g, Carbs: 5 g, Cholesterol: 88 mg, Sodium: 475 mg.

48. Coq au Riesling

Coq au Riesling is a French-inspired dish that blends the robust taste of chicken with the sweet and sour notes of Riesling wine. Served over egg noodles or mashed potatoes, this comforting dish will satisfy your taste buds.
Serving: 6
Preparation Time: 10 minutes
Ready Time: 45 minutes

Ingredients:
• 4 chicken breasts, butterflied and pounded thin
• 2 tablespoons extra-virgin olive oil
• 3 tablespoons butter
• 2 shallots, diced
• 1 cup Riesling wine
• 2 tablespoons all-purpose flour
• 1 cup chicken stock
• 2 tablespoons Dijon mustard
• 2 tablespoons honey
• 2 tablespoons chopped fresh parsley
• Salt and black pepper to taste
• Egg noodles or mashed potatoes (for serving)

Instructions:
1. Heat olive oil and butter in a large skillet over medium heat. Add in the shallots then cook until softened, about 3 minutes.
2. Add the chicken breasts and cook until golden brown, about 4-5 minutes on each side.
3. Reduce the heat to low then stir in the Riesling wine and allow it to simmer for 5 minutes.
4. In a small bowl, whisk together the flour and chicken stock until smooth.
5. Pour the flour mixture into the skillet and stir until combined.

Allow the mixture to simmer and thicken, stirring often, for 8-10 minutes.

6. Stir in the Dijon mustard, honey, parsley, and season with salt and black pepper.
7. Simmer for an additional 5 minutes.
8. Serve over egg noodles or mashed potatoes.

Nutrition information: 178 calories, 8g fat, 3g saturated fat, 14g carbohydrates, 8g protein, 567mg sodium.

49. Boulettes à la Provençale

Boulettes à la Provençale is a traditional Provençal recipe featuring delicious meatballs simmered in a flavorful tomato sauce. Beautifully seasoned with fresh herbs, this is an easy and delicious dish that the whole family will love.
Serving: 4-6
Preparation time: 30 minutes
Ready time: 1 hour

Ingredients:
- 2 tablespoons olive oil
- 1/2 onion, chopped
- 1 garlic clove, chopped
- 2 tablespoons chopped parsley
- 1/2 teaspoon fresh thyme
- 1 teaspoon chopped rosemary
- 1/2 teaspoon red pepper flakes
- 1 pound ground beef
- 2 tablespoons grated Parmesan cheese
- 2 tablespoons dry white wine
- 1 cup chicken broth
- 1 28-ounce can diced tomatoes
- 1/2 teaspoon salt
- 1/4 teaspoon freshly ground black pepper

Instructions:
1. Heat the oil in a large skillet over medium heat. Add the onion and garlic and sauté until tender, about 3 minutes.

2. Add the parsley, thyme, rosemary, and red pepper flakes and stir to combine.
3. In a large bowl, combine the ground beef, Parmesan cheese, and white wine. Form into 1-inch meatballs and add to the skillet.
4. Sauté the meatballs for 3 minutes, turning to brown on all sides.
5. Add the chicken broth, tomatoes, salt, and pepper and bring to a simmer. Simmer for 45 minutes, stirring occasionally.
6. Serve hot over cooked pasta or with crusty bread.

Nutrition information:
Serving Size: 1/6 recipe
Calories: 239
Fat: 10.2g
Cholesterol: 51mg
Sodium: 471mg
Total Carbohydrates: 10.3g
Protein: 19.8g
Fiber: 2.7g

50. Tarte au Citron

Tarte au Citron is a classic French dessert created with a tart lemon filling, encased in a buttery and flaky pastry. It is sure to be a hit with all lemon lovers!
Serving: 8
Preparation Time: 15 minutes
Ready Time: 1 hour

Ingredients:
• Refrigerated Pie Dough
• 2 large lemons
• ¾ cup of white sugar
• 1/3 cup all-purpose flour
• 2 eggs
• ¼ cup butter, melted
• 2 tablespoons of heavy cream
• 1 teaspoon of zest

Instructions:
1. Preheat the oven to 400°F. Roll out the pie dough and transfer it to a 9-inch springform pan. Trim and flute the edges with a fork.
2. Zest the lemons and cut them in half. Squeeze the juice from the lemons into the pan.
3. In a bowl, mix the sugar, flour, and eggs. Then, stir in the melted butter and heavy cream.
4. Pour this mixture into the prepared springform pan. Sprinkle the lemon zest on top.
5. Bake the tarte for about 40 minutes, or until golden brown. Let it cool completely in the pan before slicing and serving.

Nutrition information: Per serving, Tarte au Citon contains 216 calories, 9g fat, 28g carbohydrates, and 4g protein.

51. Gratin de Courgettes

Gratin de Courgettes, also known as Zucchini Gratin, is a French vegetable dish made up of thin slices of zucchini baked in cream with cheese and herbs.
Serving: 4
Preparation time: 10 minutes
Ready time: 45 minutes

Ingredients:
- 2.2 pounds (1 kg) zucchini
- 2 tablespoons butter
- 2 tablespoons olive oil
- 2 cloves garlic, minced
- 2 tablespoons all-purpose flour
- 2 cups (500 ml) heavy cream
- 2 tablespoons Parmesan cheese, grated
- 1 tablespoon fresh thyme leaves, finely chopped
- Salt and ground pepper, to taste

Instructions:
1. Preheat oven to 355°F (180°C).
2. Slice zucchini into thin rounds and set aside.

3. Heat the butter and olive oil in a skillet over medium-high heat. Add garlic and cook for 1 minute.
4. Stir in the flour and cook for another minute.
5. Gradually add cream, stirring continually. Bring the mixture to a simmer and cook for 3-5 minutes, stirring often.
6. Add Parmesan, thyme, and season with salt and pepper.
7. Grease an ovenproof dish and layer the zucchini slices in it. Pour the cream mixture over them.
8. Bake for 40-45 minutes, or until cheese is golden and bubbly.

Nutrition information: Calories: 324, Protein: 6 g, Fat: 19 g, Carbohydrates: 21.6 g, Fiber: 3 g, Sodium: 136 mg.

52. Soupe au Pistou

Soupe au Pistou is a French soup dish from Provence that combines savory vegetables, white beans, and a traditional pesto-like pistou sauce. Bursting with flavor, this comforting soup is sure to become a family favorite.
Serving: 4
Preparation Time: 10 minutes
Ready Time: 45 minutes

Ingredients:
- 3 tablespoons olive oil
- 1 large onion, chopped
- 2 cloves garlic, minced
- 2 large carrots, chopped
- 1 celery rib, chopped
- 2 cups vegetable broth
- 1 (14.5 ounce) can diced tomatoes
- 1 (15 ounce) can white beans, rinsed and drained
- 1 (4 ounce) can sliced mushrooms, drained
- 1 teaspoon dried thyme
- Salt and freshly ground black pepper
- 2 zucchini, quartered and chopped
- 1/2 cup grated Parmesan cheese
- For the Pistou Sauce:

- 2 cloves garlic
- 2 tablespoons chopped fresh basil
- 2 tablespoons chopped fresh parsley
- 2 tablespoons chopped fresh oregano
- 2 tablespoons olive oil

Instructions:
1. Heat the olive oil in a large pot over medium heat. Add the onion, garlic, carrots, and celery and cook until softened, about 5 minutes. Pour in the vegetable broth, diced tomatoes with their liquid, white beans, mushrooms, thyme, salt, and pepper. Bring to a simmer and cook for 15 minutes.
2. Meanwhile, prepare the Pistou Sauce. In a food processor, combine the garlic, basil, parsley, and oregano. Process the mixture, scraping down the sides as necessary. With the machine running, stream in the olive oil. Process until smooth.
3. Add the zucchini to the soup and cook for an additional 5 minutes.
4. Add the Pistou Sauce and Parmesan cheese to the soup. Simmer for several minutes. Serve.

Nutrition information: Calories – 231; Total Fat – 10 g; Saturated Fat – 2 g; Cholesterol – 4 mg; Sodium – 734 mg; Carbohydrate – 28 g; Protein – 8 g

53. Truite Meunière

Truite Meunière is a classic French dish of fried trout with butter and lemon. It is a great dish for seafood lovers and it is easy to make at home.
Serving: 4
Preparation Time: 10 minutes
Ready Time: 20 minutes

Ingredients:
4 (6-ounce) trout fillets,
¼ cup flour
Salt and freshly ground pepper
3 tablespoons unsalted butter
2 tablespoons freshly squeezed lemon juice

2 tablespoons finely chopped fresh parsley

Instructions:
1. Season the trout fillets with salt and pepper, then lightly dredge in the flour.
2. In a shallow skillet over medium heat, melt the butter.
3. When the butter is hot, add the trout fillets to the skillet and cook until golden brown, about 3-4 minutes per side.
4. Squeeze the lemon juice over the cooked trout and sprinkle with the parsley.
5. Serve the trout with the butter lemon sauce.

Nutrition information: Serving size: 1 fillet, Calories: 185, Fat: 9g, Carbs: 4g, Protein: 21g.

54. Confit de Canard Parmentier

Confit de Canard Parmentier is a French dish made from duck legs, potatoes, and various vegetables cooked in a pot. This classic French dish is a great meal option for a cozy evening meal with family and friends.
Serving: This recipe serves 4 people.
Preparation time: This recipe takes 30 minutes to prepare.
Ready time: This recipe takes 1 hour to cook.

Ingredients:
- 4 duck legs
- 2 tablespoons of olive oil
- 2 onions, finely chopped
- 2 cloves of garlic, minced
- 2 carrots, peeled and diced
- 2 celery stalks, diced
- 4 large potatoes, cut into cubes
- 1 bay leaf
- 1 tablespoon of fresh thyme leaves
- 2 tablespoons of tomato paste
- 2 cups of chicken broth
- Salt and pepper, to taste

Instructions:
1. Preheat oven to 375°F.
2. Heat oil in a large oven-safe pot over medium-high heat and add duck legs. Cook for 5 minutes, turning to brown on all sides.
3. Add onions, garlic, carrot, and celery and cook for another 5 minutes until vegetables start to soften. Stir in potatoes, bay leaf, thyme, tomato paste, and chicken broth. Bring to a simmer.
4. Cover pot and transfer to preheated oven. Cook for 40 minutes until potatoes are cooked through and duck legs are tender.
5. Serve and enjoy!

Nutrition information
Per serving - Calories: 489; Fat: 26.9g; Carbs: 27.2g; Protein: 30.4g

55. Terrine de Foie Gras

Terrine de Foie Gras is a classic French dish made of luxurious foie gras and aromatics, presented in a beautiful terrine. Rich in flavor and extremely delicious, it's sure to make a delicious addition to any special occasion.
Serving: Serves 8-10
Preparation Time: 10 minutes
Ready Time: 3 hours

Ingredients:
• 2 cups foie gras mousse
• 2 1/2 cups heavy cream
• 4 shallots, finely chopped
• 2 garlic cloves, minced
• 2 teaspoons dried thyme
• 2 teaspoons brandy
• 2 teaspoons Dijon mustard
• 1 teaspoon freshly ground white pepper
• 3/4 teaspoon freshly grated nutmeg
• Kosher salt, to taste
• 2 tablespoons extra-virgin olive oil
• 2-3 tablespoons Armagnac (optional)

Instructions:
1. Preheat oven to 350°F.
2. In a large bowl, whisk together Ingredients, from foie gras mousse to nutmeg.
3. Grease an 8-10 cup terrine mold with olive oil, then pour in mixture.
4. Cover terrine mold with aluminum foil and set in a roasting pan filled with enough hot water to come at least halfway up the sides of the mold.
5. Bake for 1 1/2 hours, then remove foil and bake an additional 30 minutes.
6. Remove from oven and cool. Then transfer to refrigerator to chill for at least 2 hours.
7. Serve chilled, with a drizzle of Armagnac, if desired.

Nutrition information: Per serving: 228 calories; 19 g fat; 5 g saturated fat; 253 mg cholesterol; 3 g protein; 3 g carbohydrates; 1 g sugar; 0.2 g fiber; 173 mg sodium; 88 mg calcium.

56. Gigot d'Agneau

Gigot d'Agneau is a traditional French recipe made with roasted lamb leg that can be served as either a junior, adult or shared meal.
Serving: 4
Preparation Time: 10 minutes
Ready Time: 1 1/2 hours

Ingredients:
• 4 lamb legs
• 2 tablespoons olive oil
• 2 cloves of garlic, minced
• 2 teaspoons of freshly chopped rosemary
• Salt and pepper to taste

Instructions:
1. Preheat the oven to 450°F.
2. Rub the lamb legs with olive oil and garlic and season with salt and pepper.

3. Place the lamb legs in an oven-safe dish and sprinkle with the rosemary.
4. Place the dish in the oven and roast for 1 hour and 15 minutes, flipping halfway through.
5. Remove from the oven and let cool for 5 minutes before serving.

Nutrition information: Each serving contains approximately 350 calories, 25g of fat, 2g of carbohydrates and 24g of protein.

57. Pissaladière Provençale

Pissaladière Provençale is a French flatbread tart topped with sautéed onion, anchovies, and olives originating from the Provence region of France.
Serving: 6-8
Preparation Time: 10 minutes
Ready Time: 40 minutes

Ingredients:
• 1 sheet of puff pastry, thawed
• 2 tablespoons olive oil
• 1 large onion, peeled and thinly sliced
• 3 cloves garlic, peeled and minced
• 1 teaspoon dried oregano
• ½ teaspoon sea salt
• ¼ teaspoon freshly ground black pepper
• 12 anchovy fillets, finely chopped
• ¼ cup olives, finely chopped

Instructions:
1. Preheat oven to 375°F (190°C).
2. Place the thawed puff pastry sheet onto a baking sheet.
3. Heat olive oil in a skillet over medium heat. Add onion, garlic, oregano, salt, and pepper.
4. Sauté the onion mixture for 4-5 minutes until softened.
5. Spoon the mixture onto the puff pastry sheet, spreading it out evenly.
6. Sprinkle the anchovy fillets and olives over the onion mixture.
7. Bake in the preheated oven for 25-30 minutes until the pastry is golden brown.

Nutrition information:
Calories: 135, Fat: 8g, Sugars: 1g, Protein: 3g, Carbohydrates: 13g,
Sodium: 372mg

58. Quiche Alsacienne

Quiche Alsacienne is a traditional dish from Alsace, a French region near
Germany. As a quiche dish, it's a savory custard tart that is often filled
with savory Ingredients like cheese and bacon. This delicious dish is a
classic and perfect for a light dinner or a potluck.
Serving: 8
Preparation Time: 30 minutes
Ready Time: 1 hour

Ingredients:
- On package of refrigerated pie crust
- 1/2 cup heavy cream
- 2 eggs
- 2 tablespoons of Dijon mustard
- 1/2 teaspoon of nutmeg
- 1/2 teaspoon of salt
- 1/4 teaspoon of pepper
- 1/2 cup of ham, diced
- 1 cup of shredded Swiss cheese

Instructions:
1. Preheat the oven to 375 degrees Fahrenheit.
2. Place the pie crust in a 9-inch pie plate.
3. Combine the eggs, heavy cream, mustard, nutmeg, salt, and pepper in
a large bowl and whisk until fully combined.
4. Mix in the diced ham and shredded Swiss cheese.
5. Pour the mixture into the pie plate.
6. Bake in the oven for 30 minutes, until the quiche is golden brown on
top and the center is set.
7. Let cool for 10 minutes before slicing and serving.

Nutrition information: Calories: 320 | Fat: 17g | Protein: 13g | Carbs: 25g | Fiber: 2g

59. Escargots à la Provençale

Escargots à la Provençale is a delicious French dish that is usually served as an appetizer. This delicious concoction is made with escargot, garlic, butter, and herbs that are native to Provence.
Serving: 4
Preparation Time: 15 minutes
Ready Time: 1 hour

Ingredients:
- 1 can of escargot
- 6 tablespoons of butter
- 3 cloves of garlic, minced
- 2 tablespoons of parsley, finely chopped
- 2 tablespoons of thyme, finely chopped
- Salt and pepper to taste

Instructions:
1. Preheat the oven to 350 degrees Fahrenheit.
2. Rinse the escargot and place them in a bowl.
3. In a separate bowl, mix together the butter, garlic, parsley, and thyme.
4. Divide the butter mixture into 4 equal portions.
5. Place the escargot into 4 oven safe baking dishes.
6. Top each dish with one portion of the butter mixture.
7. Bake in the oven for 15 minutes.
8. Serve the escargot hot with chopped parsley as a garnish.

Nutrition information:
Calories: 115, Fat: 9g, Sodium: 470mg, Carbohydrates: 2g, Protein: 3g.

60. Pâté en Croûte

Pâté en Croûte is a French dish consisting of fine Ingredients like mushrooms, pâté, and vegetables, all enclosed in a pastry crust. This traditional French specialty is popular for dinner parties, special occasions, and holiday feasts.

Serving: 8

Preparation time: 30 minutes

Ready time: 2 hours

Ingredients:
- 2 tablespoons unsalted butter
- 8 ounces mushrooms, chopped
- 1 diced onion
- 2 cloves garlic, minced
- Salt
- Freshly ground black pepper
- 2 teaspoons fresh thyme leaves
- 1 to 2 tablespoons brandy
- 3 tablespoons all-purpose flour
- 3/4 cup chicken broth
- 8 ounces pâté
- 2 sheets puff pastry

Instructions:
1. Preheat oven to 400 F.
2. In a large skillet, melt the butter on medium heat. Add the mushrooms, onion, garlic, salt, pepper and thyme. Cook for 2 minutes, stirring often.
3. Add the brandy to the mixture and stir for another minute, then add the flour and stir to combine. Cook for 1 minute, then add the broth and stir until mixture is thickened.
4. Divide and spread the mixture into two 9-inch pie plates. Take the pâté and divide it into 8 equal pieces. Place pâté onto the mushroom mixture in the pie plates.
5. Place puff pastry over the top of each pie plate. Using a fork, press down around the edges to seal the pastry. Cut a few holes in the top of the pastry to allow steam to escape.
6. Bake for 20 minutes. Let cool before slicing and serving.

Nutrition information:
Calories: 294

Fat: 14.3g

Saturated Fat: 5.1g

Cholesterol: 29mg
Sodium: 517mg
Carbohydrates: 23.4g
Fiber: 2.6g
Sugar: 1.3g
Protein: 12.8g

61. Rillettes de Porc

Rillettes de Porc is a delicious French delicacy of pork pâté that is slowly cooked with herbs and spices. It is a shredded pork dish that is perfect to enjoy at any time of year.
Serving: 4
Preparation Time: 25 minutes
Ready Time: 3-4 hrs

Ingredients:
-750 grams of pork shoulder
-1 large onion
-2 cloves garlic
-50 ml of cognac
-50 ml of white wine
-1 tablespoon of olive oil
-2 tablespoons of fresh thyme
-2 tablespoons of fresh parsley
-1 bay leaf
-Salt and pepper to taste

Instructions:
1. Preheat oven to 180°C.
2. In a large oven-proof dish, layer the onion, garlic and pork shoulder.
3. Drizzle cognac and wine over the meat.
4. Sprinkle thyme, parsley, bay leaf, olive oil, salt and pepper over the meat.
5. Place in preheated oven and cook for 3-4 hours, uncovered.
6. When cooked, shred the pork gently with two forks.
7. Serve warm or cold with crusty bread and pickles.

Nutrition information: Each serving of Rillettes de Porc contains 161 calories, 5.7 g fat, 0.6 g saturated fat, 12.2 g protein, and 4.3 g carbohydrates.

62. Boulettes de Veau à la Crème

Boulettes de veau à la crème is a sumptuous dish originating from northern France. Traditionally made of veal mince mixed with spices and fresh herbs, it is slow-cooked in a creamy white sauce.
Serving: Serves 6
Preparation Time: 1 hour
Ready time: 1 hour and 30 minutes

Ingredients:
- 500g minced veal
- 1 onion, finely chopped
- 1 clove garlic, finely chopped
- 1 egg
- 2 tablespoons freshly chopped parsley
- 1 teaspoon thyme
- 1 teaspoon rosemary
- 1 teaspoon sea salt
- 2 tablespoons olive oil
- 200ml double cream
- 150ml vegetable stock

Instructions:
1. In a large bowl, mix the minced veal, onion, garlic, egg, herbs, and salt.
2. Beat the mixture until it is a homogeneous blend.
3. Use your hands to form small, oval-shaped patties out of the mixture.
4. Heat the olive oil in a large pan over medium-high heat.
5. Add the patties to the pan and cook until golden brown, about 3-4 minutes per side.
6. When the patties are cooked, transfer them to a plate and set aside.
7. Add the double cream and vegetable stock to the pan and reduce the heat to medium-low. Simmer the sauce for about 10 minutes, stirring occasionally.
8. Return the patties to the pan and gently toss them in the sauce.

9. Serve the Boulettes de Veau à la Crème with boiled potatoes, steamed vegetables, or crusty bread.

Nutrition information: per serving – Calories: 391, Fat: 23g, Carbohydrates: 4.3g, Protein: 33g

63. Caille en Sarcophage

Caille en Sarcophage is a classic French dish that is typically served during the holidays. It is composed of a stuffed quail cooked in pastry that is usually shaped like a coffin.
Serving: 6
Preparation Time: 45 minutes
Ready Time: 1 hour

Ingredients:
- 6 quail
- 5.3 ounces of foie gras
- 1.7 ounces of lean ham
- 1 small onion, chopped
- 2 cloves of garlic, minced
- 4 tablespoons of chopped parsley
- Salt and pepper to taste
- 4 tablespoons of butter
- 2 tablespoons of olive oil
- 2 sheets of puff pastry

Instructions:
1. Preheat the oven to 350 degrees F.
2. In a skillet, heat the butter and olive oil over medium heat.
3. Add the onion, garlic, parsley, salt, and pepper and cook for 5 minutes, stirring occasionally.
4. Add the foie gras and ham and cook for 5 more minutes, stirring occasionally.
5. Stuff the quail with the observed mixture and close the flap of each quail with a wooden skewer.
6. Cut the puff pastry into circles large enough to wrap around each quail.

7. Place the quail on the puff pastry, fold it to close the parcel, and seal it with a dab of water or egg white.
8. Place the parcels on a baking tray leaving space between them.
9. Bake for 40 minutes.
10. Transfer to a serving platter and serve.

Nutrition information: Each parcel contains approximately 451 calories, 31 g of fat, 20 g of carbohydrates, and 21 g of protein.

64. Daube de Boeuf

Daube de Boeuf, or beef daube, is a rich and flavorful French beef stew. It is slowly braised in red wine with herbs and vegetables to create a perfect comforting winter dinner.
Serving: 4
Preparation Time: 15 minutes
Ready Time: 4 hours

Ingredients:
- 2-3 pounds of stewing beef
- 2 tablespoons of oil
- 1 large onion, diced
- 3 cloves of garlic, minced
- 2 carrots, peeled and diced
- 2 stalks of celery, diced
- 1 cup of red wine
- 1 can of diced tomatoes
- 1 teaspoon of thyme
- 1 teaspoon of herbes de provence
- Salt and pepper, to taste

Instructions:
1. Heat the oil in a large pot over medium-high heat. Add the beef and cook for 5 minutes, until browned.
2. Add the onion, garlic, carrot, and celery and cook for 5 minutes.
3. Pour in the wine and reduce the heat. Simmer for 10 minutes, until the liquid is reduced by half.
4. Add the tomatoes, thyme, herbes de provence, salt, and pepper.

5. Reduce the heat to low and simmer uncovered for 3 hours, stirring occasionally.
6. Serve over mashed potatoes or with crusty bread.

Nutrition information: Calories: 250, Fat: 8 g, Carbs: 16 g, Protein: 20 g

65. Gougères

Introduce Gougères as a savory pastry typical of French cuisine
Serving: Makes around 30
Preparation time: 10 minutes
Ready time: 20 minutes

Ingredients:
2 large eggs, 4 ounces (1 stick) of butter, ¼ cup of water, ¼ teaspoon of salt, 1 cup of all purpose flour, 5 ounces of Gruyère cheese

Instructions:
1. Preheat the oven to 375 degrees and line a baking sheet with parchment paper.
2. In a small saucepan over medium heat, melt the butter with the water and salt.
3. Once the butter has melted, bring it to a simmer, then turn off the heat and add the flour all at once.
4. Using a wooden spoon, stir the flour until it comes together and forms a ball.
5. Transfer the dough to a bowl and let cool for 5 minutes.
6. Beat in the eggs one at a time, stirring until the dough is glossy and smooth.
7. Stir in the cheese and mix until it's well combined.
8. Drop tablespoon-sized balls of dough onto the parchment lined baking sheet.
9. Bake for 15-20 minutes until golden brown.
10. Serve warm.

Nutrition information: 50 calories per serving, 5g fat, 3g protein, 1.5g carbohydrates

66. Pommes Duchesse

Not to be confused with mashed potatoes, Pommes Duchesse is a traditional French side dish of spiced potatoes whipped and lightened with egg.
Serving: 4-6
Preparation Time: 30 minutes
Ready Time: 45 minutes

Ingredients:
- 8 large potatoes
- 2 large eggs
- 2 tablespoons butter
- 1/4 teaspoon nutmeg
- Salt and pepper
- 1 tablespoon parsley (optional)

Instructions:
1. Preheat oven to 375°F.
2. Peel the potatoes and cook in boiling salted water for 25 minutes or until tender.
3. Drain potatoes and mash thoroughly.
4. Beat in the eggs, butter, and nutmeg, making it into a smooth mix.
5. Season with salt and pepper.
6. Scoop the mix with a spoon and shape into small, round mounds on a greased baking sheet.
7. Bake for 15 minutes or until golden.
8. Garnish with parsley before serving.

Nutrition information:
Calories: 125, Fat: 4.5g, Sodium: 30mg, Carbohydrates: 17.3g, Protein: 3.5g

67. Chou Farci

Chou Farci is a delicious French vegetable dish, commonly known as stuffed cabbage or cabbage roll. It has a savory filling of herbs and meat, all wrapped up in a tender, cooked cabbage leaf.
Serving: 6-8
Preparation Time: 20 minutes
Ready Time: 45 minutes

Ingredients:
- 1 large head cabbage
- 1 pound lean ground beef
- ¼ cup minced onion
- 1 egg
- 1 teaspoon salt
- 1 teaspoon black pepper
- ¼ teaspoon ground nutmeg
- ½ cup cooked rice
- 2 tablespoons olive oil
- 2 cans (14.5 ounces each) tomato sauce

Instructions:
1. Preheat oven to 350 degrees F.
2. Remove 12 outer cabbage leaves; set aside. Cut off top of cabbage and reserve. Cut out a core from the bottom of the cabbage and discard.
3. In a large mixing bowl, combine beef, onion, egg, salt, pepper, nutmeg and cooked rice. Gently mix with your hands until all Ingredients are combined.
4. Place a scant ½ cup of the meat mixture in the center of each of the reserved cabbage leaves and roll up.
5. Place cabbage rolls in a large baking dish and top with the top of the cabbage and the tomato sauce. Cover baking dish with aluminum foil.
6. Bake for 45 minutes in preheated oven.

Nutrition information: Calories: 256, Total Fat: 11.7g, Saturated Fat: 3.2g, Trans Fat: 0.0g, Cholesterol: 61mg, Sodium: 871mg, Carbohydrates: 18.5g, Fiber: 4.1g, Sugar: 8.6g, Protein: 18.7g.

68. Gratin de Macaroni

Gratin de Macaroni is an easy and delicious pasta dish made with traditional Italian flavors like garlic, onion, tomatoes and herbs. The dish is hearty and creamy, and it is sure to be a crowd pleaser.
Serving: 6
Preparation time: 20 minutes
Ready time: 30 minutes

Ingredients:
- 12 ounces of macaroni pasta
- 1 tablespoon of olive oil
- 1 onion, chopped
- 2 cloves of garlic, minced
- 2 tablespoons of butter
- 2 tablespoons of all-purpose flour
- 1 teaspoon of Italian seasoning
- 2 cups of whole milk
- 1 cup of grated Parmesan cheese
- 2 cups of shredded mozzarella cheese
- 1 can (14.5 ounces) of diced tomatoes
- 1/4 cup of chopped parsley

Instructions:
1. Preheat oven to 375°F.
2. Bring a large pot of salted water to a boil. Add macaroni pasta and cook for 6 minutes or until al dente. Drain and set aside.
3. Heat olive oil in a large skillet over medium-high heat. Add onion and garlic and cook for 3 minutes, stirring occasionally.
4. Reduce heat to medium-low and add butter to the pan. Once the butter has melted, add flour and Italian seasoning and stir until combined. Gradually add milk, whisking constantly until the mixture is smooth and thick.
5. Add Parmesan and mozzarella cheeses and stir until cheese is melted. Add diced tomatoes and parsley and stir until combined.
6. Add the cooked macaroni to the skillet and stir until the macaroni is coated with the cheese mixture.
7. Transfer the macaroni mixture to a 9x13 inch baking dish. Sprinkle with remaining Parmesan cheese and bake for 15 minutes or until cheese is golden and bubbly.
8. Let rest for 5 minutes before serving.

Nutrition information: 420 Calories; 20 g of Fat; 20 mg of Cholesterol; 320 mg of Sodium; 34 g of Carbohydrate; 3 g of Fiber; 12 g of Protein.

69. Parmentier de Canard

Parmentier de canard is a classic French casserole, combining shredded duck, potatoes, and creamy cheese sauce for a perfect comforting dish.
Serving: 6
Preparation time: 15 minutes
Ready time: 45 minutes

Ingredients:
- 2 tablespoons of olive oil
- 400g shredded duck
- 2 large potatoes, thinly sliced
- 1 onion, finely chopped
- 2 cloves garlic, minced
- 2 tablespoons fresh thyme leaves
- 200ml vegetable stock
- 200ml single cream
- 100g gruyere cheese
- Salt and pepper, to taste

Instructions:
1. Preheat the oven to 190°C.
2. Heat the olive oil in a large oven-proof casserole dish. Add the duck, potatoes, onion, garlic and thyme and cook for 10 minutes until lightly golden.
3. Pour in the vegetable stock and cream and simmer for 10 minutes, stirring occasionally.
4. Sprinkle over the cheese and season to taste before baking in the oven for 20-25 minutes until golden and bubbling.
5. Serve immediately.

Nutrition information: per serving – calories: 445, protein: 18g, fat: 25g, carbohydrates: 24g

70. Mousse au Chocolat

Mousse au Chocolat is an irresistible French classic made of smooth and silky chocolate.
Serving: 4
Preparation Time: 30 minutes
Ready Time: 4 hours

Ingredients:
150 g dark chocolate, plus extra for topping
180 ml double cream
3 large eggs
3 tbsp icing sugar

Instructions:
1. Place the chopped chocolate in a heatproof bowl over a pan of simmering water. Heat until fully melted and set aside to cool.
2. In a separate bowl, whip the double cream to soft peaks and set aside.
3. Separate the eggs, ensuring no yolk gets into the whites.
4. Whisk the egg whites with the icing sugar until stiff peaks form.
5. Gently fold the melted chocolate into the egg whites using a rubber spatula.
6. Fold in the whipped cream.
7. Divide the mousse between four glasses and top with some extra chopped chocolate.
8. Place in the refrigerator for at least 4 hours to set.
 Nutrition information: 230 Calories, 16g Fat, 19g Carbohydrates, 3g Protein

71. Caramelized Onion and Gruyère Tart

This savory tart is a delicious combination of sweet caramelized onions and creamy Gruyère cheese. It makes a great appetizer or main dish for brunch or lunch.
Serving: Serves 6.
Preparation Time
15 minutes

Ready time: 35 minutes

Ingredients:
- 2 tablespoons olive oil
- 2 medium-sized onions, thinly sliced
- 1 refrigerated rolled sheet of short crust pastry
- 1/4 cup sour cream
- 1/2 cup Gruyère cheese, grated
- 2 tablespoons cream cheese
- Salt and pepper, to taste

Instructions:
1. Preheat oven to 375 °F (190 °C).
2. Heat oil in a skillet over medium heat and sauté onions for 10 minutes or until caramelized.
3. Unroll pastry sheet onto a baking tray lined with parchment paper.
4. Spread sour cream in the center of the pastry, leaving a 1-inch border.
5. Top with caramelized onions, Gruyère cheese, and cream cheese.
6. Sprinkle with salt and pepper.
7. Bake for 15-20 minutes or until pastry is golden brown.

Nutrition information
Per serving (1/6 tart): 256 calories, 15.4g fat, 16.6g carbohydrates, 9.2g protein

72. Crêpes Suzette

Crêpes Suzette is a classic French dessert made with thin pancakes, butter, sugar, and orange liqueur.
Serving: 6
Preparation time: 30 minutes
Ready time: 25 minutes

Ingredients:
- 1 ½ cups all-purpose flour
- 3 eggs
- 2 cups milk
- ½ cup unsalted butter
- ¼ cup granulated sugar

- 1 teaspoon vanilla extract
- 1 teaspoon orange zest
- 2 tablespoons Grand Marnier or other orange liqueur

Instructions:
1. In a large bowl, whisk together flour and eggs until smooth. Slowly add milk, whisking until all the milk is incorporated and the batter is smooth.
2. Melt butter in a large skillet over medium heat. Once the butter has melted, pour the batter into the skillet, using a ¼ cup measure for each crepe.
3. Cook each crepe for 2 minutes, or until edges are starting to turn golden. Flip crepes and cook for another 1 minute. Remove from skillet and place on a plate.
4. Melt the remaining ½ cup of butter in the skillet. Sprinkle on the granulated sugar and stir until the mixture starts to bubble. Add the orange liqueur and orange zest and simmer for 1 minute.
5. Return crepes to the skillet and spoon the sauce over the top. Baste each crepe with the sauce and cook for 2 minutes per side. Serve warm.

Nutrition information: 417 calories, 23g fat, 33g carbohydrates, 7g protein

73. Blanquette de Veau à l'Ancienne

Blanquette de Veau à l'Ancienne is a French veal stew that is savory and flavorful. It is usually served with pasta, egg noodles or boiled potatoes.
Serving: 6
Preparation time: 30 minutes
Ready time: 1 hour 30 minutes

Ingredients:
- 2 lbs of veal stew meat
- 2 tablespoons of butter
- 2 tablespoons of flour
- 2 cups of beef broth
- 1 medium onion, diced
- 2 tablespoons of flour

- 2 tablespoons of tomato paste
- 2 tablespoons of white wine
- 2 tablespoons of freshly minced parsley
- 2 tablespoons of freshly minced chives
- 1/2 teaspoon of sea salt
- 1/2 teaspoon of freshly ground black pepper

Instructions:
1. In a large Dutch oven, melt butter over medium heat.
2. Add the veal cubes and brown lightly.
3. Remove the veal cubes from the pan and set aside.
4. To the same pot, add the diced onions, tomato paste, and flour. Cook until the onions are soft and lightly browned, about 5 minutes.
5. Add the beef broth, white wine, parsley, chives, sea salt and ground black pepper. return the veal cubes to the pot and bring the mixture to a boil.
6. Reduce the heat to low and simmer for 1 hour.
7. Serve the stew with cooked noodles, pasta, or boiled potatoes.

Nutrition information:
Calories: 485, Fat: 17 g, Carbs: 32 g, Protein: 48 g, Cholesterol: 146 mg, Sodium: 545 mg, Sugar: 2 g

74 Soufflé au Fromage

Soufflé au Fromage (or Cheese Soufflé) is a timeless French classic. With its creamy texture and rich flavor, it is perfect for weekend brunch, a posh dinner party, or just a cozy night at home.
Serving: 4
Preparation Time: 15 minutes
Ready Time: 45 minutes

Ingredients:
- 3 ½ tbsp. butter
- 2 tbsp. all-purpose flour
- 2/3 cup warm milk
- 2/3 cup shredded Gruyere or Emmenthal cheese
- 4 eggs, separated
- Pinch freshly grated nutmeg

- Pinch cayenne pepper
- 2 ½ tbsp. fresh parsley, chopped

Instructions:
1. Preheat oven to 425°F. Grease a 4-cup soufflé dish with 1 ½ tablespoon butter and lightly dust with flour.
2. Melt remaining 2 tablespoons of butter in a large saucepan over medium-high heat. Whisk in flour, and cook for 1-2 minutes until lightly golden. Remove from heat and add warm milk, stirring constantly with a wooden spoon as the mixture thickens.
3. Stir in cheese until melted, then season with nutmeg and cayenne pepper.
4. In a large bowl with an electric mixer, beat egg whites until stiff peaks form.
5. Gently fold egg whites into cheese mixture.
6. Pour into prepared dish and sprinkle with remaining 2 tablespoons butter and chopped parsley.
7. Bake in preheated oven for 25-35 minutes until risen and lightly golden. Serve immediately.

Nutrition information: Per serving, 200 calories, 15 g fat, 8 g saturated fat, 7 g carbohydrates, 9 g protein, and 430 mg sodium.

75. Far Breton

Far Breton is a classic French dessert made with eggs, sugar, milk, flour, and prunes. It is a delicious comfort food that's great for snacking, breakfast, or dessert.
Serving: Serves 8
Preparation Time: 20 minutes
Ready Time: 1 hour

Ingredients:
• 8-10 prunes, chopped
• 2 cups whole milk
• 3 eggs
• ½ cup sugar
• ½ cup all-purpose flour

- 2 tablespoons butter, melted
- Powdered sugar, as desired

Instructions:
1. Preheat oven to 350°F (175°C).
2. Grease an 8-inch or 9-inch baking pan.
3. Place chopped prunes in the bottom of the pan.
4. In a bowl, whisk together milk, eggs, sugar, and flour until combined.
5. Pour the mixture over the prunes.
6. Drizzle melted butter on top.
7. Place in oven and bake for 40-50 minutes, until the top is golden brown and a knife inserted in the middle comes out clean.
8. Cool for 10 minutes before serving.
9. Dust with powdered sugar and enjoy!

Nutrition information:
Calories: 172 kcal, Carbohydrates: 22 g, Protein: 4 g, Fat: 8 g, Saturated Fat: 2 g, Cholesterol: 44 mg, Sodium: 39 mg, Potassium: 181 mg, Fiber: 1 g, Sugar: 15 g, Vitamin A: 252 IU, Calcium: 56 mg, Iron: 1 mg.

76. Escargots en Croute

Escargots en Croute is a classic French dish featuring snails cooked in a pastry crust.
Serving: 6
Preparation time: 10 min
Ready time: 45 min

Ingredients:
- 24 snails
- 8 oz butter
- 4 cloves garlic, minced
- 2 shallots, minced
- 1 ¼ cups dry white wine
- 2 tablespoons parsley, minced
- 6 sheets pre-made puff pastry

Instructions:

1. Preheat oven to 350 degrees F (176 degrees C).
2. In a pan over medium-high heat, melt the butter. Add the garlic and shallots, cooking until softened.
3. Then add the snails, parsley, and wine. Simmer for 6 minutes.
4. On a lightly floured surface, roll out the puff pastry sheet until it is 14 inches by 14 inches and 1/4 inch thick. Cut into 6 equal squares.
5. Place a small amount of the snail mixture in the center of each square. Fold the squares in half, forming a triangle. Press the edges together using a fork.
6. Place the triangles on a baking sheet and bake for 20 minutes, or until the pastry is golden.

Nutrition information: Per Serving: 639 calories, 40.1g fat, 15.4g carbohydrates, 38.5g protein

77. Salade Lyonnaise

Salade Lyonnaise is a classic French salad with crunchy pieces of bacon, a poached egg, and warm vinaigrette. This dish is a delightful balance of flavors, combining savory and slightly sweet Ingredients.
Serving: 6
Preparation time: 10 minutes
Ready time: 15 minutes

Ingredients:
-6 slices of bacon
-6 eggs
-6 ounce cucumber
-2 stalks of celery
-2 tablespoons of olive oil
-2 tablespoons of balsamic vinegar
-2 tablespoons of Dijon mustard
-1 teaspoon of sugar
-Salt and pepper to taste

Instructions:

1. Start by cooking the bacon in a large skillet over medium heat until crispy. Remove bacon from the skillet and place on a plate lined with paper towels.

2. Once the bacon is cooked, poach the eggs by filling a saucepan with about two inches of water and bringing it to a boil. Once boiling, reduce the heat to a simmer and carefully break the eggs into the simmering water. Cook for 2-3 minutes, until the whites are set but the yolks are still runny. Carefully remove eggs from the saucepan and set aside.

3. Thinly slice the cucumber and celery and place in a large bowl.

4. To make the vinaigrette, mix the olive oil, balsamic vinegar, Dijon mustard, and sugar together in a jar. Shake until it is well blended, then season with salt and pepper to taste.

5. Place the bacon, poached eggs, and vinaigrette in the bowl with the cucumber and celery and toss until the Ingredients are evenly coated. Serve the Salade Lyonnaise immediately.

Nutrition information (per serving): 220 calories, 20g fat, 5g carbohydrates, 10g protein.

78. Pâté de Foie

Pâté de Foie is a classic French delicacy made using duck or chicken livers which are simmered in a classic white sauce made with brandy and clarified butter. This dish is smooth and flavorful, and can be spread on bread or served with crackers or vegetables.

Serving: 8
Preparation time: 10 minutes
Ready time: 25 minutes

Ingredients:
-8 ounces duck or chicken liver
-2 tablespoons brandy
-4 tablespoons clarified butter
-3 tablespoons minced shallots
-1/4 teaspoon dried thyme
-2 tablespoons heavy cream
-Salt and pepper to taste

Instructions:

1. Rinse the livers under cold water and pat dry.
2. Heat the clarified butter in a medium skillet over medium heat.
3. Add the minced shallots and cook until softened, about 2-3 minutes.
4. Add the livers and cook until lightly browned, about 3-5 minutes.
5. Add the brandy and cook for an additional 2 minutes.
6. Remove from heat and let cool for 5 minutes.
7. Add the cooked liver mixture, thyme, and heavy cream to a food processor and blend until smooth.
8. Season with salt and pepper to taste.

Nutrition information: Serving size: 1/8 of recipe. Calories: 150, Fat: 13g, Carbs: 2g, Protein: 5g.

79. Brandade de Morue à la Provençale

Brandade de Morue à la Provençale is a traditional Provençal dish featuring salt cod. It is a delicious and creamy potato-based dish made with garlic, onion, and olive oil, making the dish light and savory.
Serving: 6
Preparation Time: 15 minutes
Ready Time: More than an hour

Ingredients:
1 lb unsalted salt cod
1 lb potatoes, peeled and quartered
3 cloves garlic, diced
1/2 onion diced
1/2 cup olive oil
3 tablespoons parsley, minced
2 tablespoons fresh thyme leaves
2 tablespoons lemon juice
1 teaspoon ground black pepper

Instructions:
1. Rinse the salt cod and place in a pot filled with cold water. Bring to a boil and cook until tender, about 10 minutes. Drain and shred the cod with a fork.

2. Bring a pot of salted water to a boil and add the potatoes. Boil until tender, about 20 minutes. Drain and mash the potatoes with a fork or potato ricer.

3. In a large saucepan, heat the olive oil over medium heat. Add the garlic and onion and cook until soft, about 5 minutes.

4. Reduce the heat to low and add the mashed potatoes, salt cod, parsley, thyme and lemon juice. Stir to combine and heat through for 5 minutes.

5. Add the ground pepper and stir to combine. Cook for an additional 5 minutes and serve.

Nutrition information: Servings: 6 | Calories: 252 kcal | Carbohydrates: 9 g | Protein: 14 g | Fat: 16 g | Sodium: 1273 mg | Potassium: 465 mg | Fiber: 2 g | Sugar: 1 g | Vitamin A: 483 IU | Vitamin C: 9 mg | Calcium: 81 mg | Iron: 4 mg

80. Fougasse

Fougasse is a traditional French bread that is crunchy, light and airy. It is the perfect addition to soups, salads and other dishes.

Serving: Serves 4
Preparation Time: 30 minutes
Ready Time: 1 hour 15 minutes

Ingredients:
- 3 3/4 cups all-purpose flour
- 1 teaspoon salt
- 2 teaspoons active dry yeast
- 1/4 cup olive oil
- 1 1/4 cups warm water
- Herbs and spices (optional)

Instructions:
1. In a bowl, combine the flour, salt and yeast.

2. Add the olive oil and warm water to the flour mixture and stir until the dough starts to form.

3. Knead the dough on a floured surface for about 10 minutes until the dough is smooth and elastic.

4. Place the dough in a greased bowl and cover with a damp cloth. Let it rise in a warm place for about an hour.
5. Divide the dough into four equal pieces, making four round balls and flatten them lightly.
6. Take one ball and form it into an oval shape and pinch the sides in the middle to create a slit in the bread.
7. Place the fougasse on a lightly greased baking sheet and let it rise for about 15 minutes.
8. Preheat the oven to 400°F and bake the fougasse for 15-20 minutes until it turns golden brown.

Nutrition information: Per serving: 285 Calories, 4g Total Fat, 0g Saturated Fat, 0mg Cholesterol, 583mg Sodium, 169mg Potassium, 58g Carbohydrates, 5g Dietary Fiber, 3g Sugars, 8g Protein.

81. Tarte aux Poireaux

Tarte aux Poireaux is a French savory tart made with leeks, Gruyère cheese, and a creamy custard. It is a flavorful dish that is perfect for brunch, lunch, or dinner.
Serving: 8
Preparation time: 20 minutes
Ready time: 45 minutes

Ingredients:
- 2 tablespoons butter
- 2 leeks, washed and sliced
- 2 tablespoons flour
- 2 cups whole milk
- 4 eggs
- 2 tablespoons Dijon mustard
- 8 ounces Gruyère cheese, grated
- Salt and pepper, to taste
- 1 store-bought tart crust

Instructions:
1. Preheat the oven to 400°F.

2. In a large skillet, melt the butter over medium heat and then add the leeks. Cook for 6-7 minutes, until the leeks are softened.
3. In a medium bowl, whisk together the flour and milk.
4. In a separate bowl, whisk together the eggs, Dijon mustard, Gruyère cheese, and salt and pepper.
5. Add the milk-flour mixture to the egg-cheese mixture and whisk together until combined.
6. Spread the leeks into the store-bought tart crust. Pour the custard mixture over the leeks.
7. Bake for 25 minutes, until the custard is set. Let cool for 10 minutes before serving.

Nutrition information (per serving):
Calories: 253; Fat: 16g; Protein: 12g; Total Carbohydrates: 15.2g; Dietary Fiber: 0.9g; Sodium: 208mg

82. Poulet à la Crème

This delicious French classic, Poulet à la Crème, is an easy and creamy indulgence. The dish consists of tender chicken cooked in a rich and creamy sauce, with plenty of herbs and seasonings.
Serving: 4
Preparation time: 10 minutes
Ready time: 25 minutes

Ingredients:
•2 tablespoons butter
•4 boneless and skinless chicken breasts
•1 onion, finely chopped
•200ml single cream
•2 tablespoons lemon juice
•1 tablespoon fresh chopped parsley
•1 teaspoon fresh marjoram
•Salt and pepper to taste

Instructions:
1.Heat the butter in a skillet over medium-high heat.
2.Season the chicken breasts with salt and pepper.

3.Add the chicken to the skillet and cook for 8 minutes, or until golden brown and cooked through.
4.Remove the chicken from the skillet and set aside.
5.Add the chopped onion to the skillet and cook for 5 minutes.
6.Stir in the single cream, lemon juice, parsley and marjoram.
7.Bring the mixture to a gentle simmer.
8.Return the chicken to the skillet and simmer for 8 minutes.
9.Serve hot with your favourite side dishes.

Nutrition information:
Calories: 400 kcal
Carbohydrates: 5g
Protein: 30g
Fat: 25g

83. Boulettes de Porc aux Herbes

Boulettes de porc aux herbes is a classic French-style pork dish originating from the Provence region of France. It is a flavorful, savory preparation of ground pork enhanced with herbs and spices. Servings: 4 Preparation Time: 20 minutes Ready Time: 40 minutes

Ingredients:
1 lb ground pork, 2 eggs, 2 cloves garlic, minced, 2 tablespoons parsley, minced, 1 teaspoon fresh thyme, minced, 3 tablespoons breadcrumbs, 1 teaspoon onion powder, 1 teaspoon ground cumin, 1/2 teaspoon nutmeg, 1/2 teaspoon sea salt, 2 tablespoons olive oil

Instructions:
1. In a large bowl, combine ground pork, eggs, garlic, parsley, thyme, breadcrumbs, onion powder, cumin, nutmeg, and salt. Use your hands to combine all of the Ingredients, making sure everything is well combined.
2. Wet your hands and form the mixture into equal-sized meatballs.
3. Heat the olive oil in a large skillet over medium heat.
4. Once the oil is hot, add the meatballs to the skillet and cook for 10-12 minutes, gently turning them as needed to ensure they are evenly cooked.
5. Once the meatballs are cooked, remove them from the heat and serve.

Nutrition information: Per Serving: cal: 298 fat: 20.5g carbs: 5g protein: 23.5g sodium: 251mg sugar: 0.5g

84. Cassoulet Toulousain

Cassoulet Toulousain is a country-style French dish from the city of Toulouse. This hearty one-pot meal consists of white beans simmered in a rich broth along with pork, duck and sausages.
Serving: Serves 4
Preparation time: 10 minutes
Ready time: 3 hours

Ingredients:
• 2 tablespoons olive oil
• 1 onion, chopped
• 2 cloves garlic, minced
• 1 large carrot, diced
• 2 stalks celery, chopped
• 1/4 teaspoon thyme leaves
• 1 tablespoon tomato paste
• 6 cups chicken broth
• 1 pound dried white beans, soaked overnight
• 2 smoked pork hocks
• 2 smoked duck legs
• 1/2 pound of garlic sausage, cut into 1-inch pieces
• 2 tablespoons chopped parsley
• Salt and black pepper to taste

Instructions:
1. Heat the olive oil in a large Dutch oven or pot over medium-high heat. Add the onion, garlic, carrot, and celery and cook, stirring often, until the vegetables are soft, about 5 minutes.
2. Add the thyme and tomato paste and cook, stirring, for 2 minutes.
3. Add the chicken broth and the soaked white beans. Add the pork hocks, duck legs, and sausage.
4. Bring the mixture to a boil, reduce the heat to low, and simmer, covered, stirring occasionally, until the beans are tender and the liquid has thickened, about 2 hours.

5. Remove the pork hocks and duck legs and discard the bones and fat. Return the meat to the pot.
6. Stir in the parsley, season with salt and pepper, and cook for another 30 minutes.
7. Serve the cassoulet with crusty bread or rice.

Nutrition information:
Calories 230, Total fat 8 g, Cholesterol 38 mg, Sodium 309 mg, Potassium 595 mg, Total carbohydrate 24 g, Protein 15 g.

85. Mussels in White Wine Sauce

This easy and delicious recipe for mussels in white wine sauce is sure to transport you to Mediterranean shores! White wine brings out the sweetness of the mussels, combined with garlic and shallots for an amazing flavor.
Serving: Serves 4
Preparation time: 10 minutes
Ready time: 20 minutes

Ingredients:
• 2 tablespoons olive oil
• 2 cloves garlic, minced
• 1 large shallot, minced
• 1 cup (250 mL) white wine
• 2 pounds (1 kg) fresh mussels, scrubbed and debearded
• 2 tablespoons parsley, chopped
• Salt and pepper to taste

Instructions:
1. Heat the olive oil in a large pot over medium heat.
2. Add garlic and shallot and sauté for about 5 minutes until softened.
3. Pour in the white wine and bring to a simmer.
4. Add the mussels, cover the pot, and cook for about 5 minutes until mussels open.
5. Sprinkle the parsley, season with salt and pepper, and give everything a good stir.
6. Serve and enjoy!

Nutrition information: Nutritional information for one serving is not available, however, mussels are low in fat and calories and a good source of protein and iron.

86. Pain Perdu

Pain Perdu which literally translates to "lost bread" is a popular French dessert made by soaking dry, stale bread in milk, eggs, and sugar then pan-frying until golden brown.
Serving: 4
Preparation Time: 20 minutes
Ready Time: 30 minutes

Ingredients:
4-6 slices of dry, stale bread
1 cup of whole milk
2 eggs
1 teaspoon of vanilla extract
2 tablespoons of sugar
3 tablespoons of butter

Instructions:
1. Cover the bread slices with the milk and let sit for 10 minutes for the bread to soak up the liquid.
2. In a separate bowl, mix together the eggs, vanilla extract and sugar until fully blended.
3. Heat a large frying pan over medium-high heat and melt the butter.
4. Dip each slice of bread into the egg mixture, coating each side.
5. Place the coated bread slices into the pan and cook for about 3-5 minutes on each side, or until golden-brown.
6. Serve hot with ice cream or your favorite topping.

Nutrition information:
Calories: 282 calories, Protein: 9g, Fat: 13g, Sodium: 258mg, Carbohydrates: 31g, Sugar: 13g.

87. Côtelettes d'Agneau

Côtelettes d'Agneau is a classic French dish made of French-style grilled lamb chops. This traditional dish is easy to make and packed with flavor.
Serving: 4
Preparation Time: 15 minutes
Ready Time: 15 minutes

Ingredients:
• 4 bone-in lamb chops
• 4 teaspoons olive oil
• 2 tablespoons of garlic, chopped
• 2 teaspoons fresh rosemary, chopped
• 2 teaspoons fresh thyme, chopped
• 1 teaspoon fresh oregano, chopped
• 1 teaspoon sea salt
• 1 teaspoon freshly ground pepper

Instructions:
1. Preheat the grill to high heat or stovetop griddle to medium-high heat.
2. Rub the lamb chops with 1 tablespoon of the olive oil.
3. In a small bowl, mix together the garlic, rosemary, thyme, oregano, salt and pepper to create the marinade.
4. Generously season the lamb chops with the marinade.
5. Place the chops on the grill or griddle and cook for 3 to 4 minutes on each side, or until desired doneness.
6. Remove the lamb chops from the heat and let sit for 5 minutes before serving.

Nutrition information:
• Calories: 256 calories
• Fat: 13.7 grams
• Protein: 28.3 grams
• Carbs: 0.8 grams

88. Ratatouille Tart

Ratatouille Tart is a French-inspired dish made of colorful vegetables, herbs, and a flavorful cheese-based topping. It is a delicious, healthy, and vegetarian-friendly option that's easy to make.

Serving: 8
Preparation Time: 10 minutes
Ready Time: 45 minutes

Ingredients:
- 2 tablespoons olive oil
- 2 onions, finely chopped
- 2 cloves garlic, finely chopped
- 1 red bell pepper, finely chopped
- 1 yellow bell pepper, finely chopped
- 1 eggplant, diced
- 2 zucchini, diced
- 2 tablespoons fresh thyme leaves
- 2 teaspoons fresh oregano leaves
- Salt and pepper, to taste
- ½ cup tomato passata
- 1 sheet pre-rolled shortcrust pastry
- 1½ cups grated cheddar cheese

Instructions:
1. Preheat the oven to 375°F/190°C.
2. Heat the oil in a large non-stick skillet over medium-high heat. Add the onion and garlic and cook for 5 minutes, stirring occasionally.
3. Add the bell peppers, eggplant, zucchini, thyme, oregano, salt, and pepper. Cook for 7–10 minutes or until the vegetables are tender.
4. Add the passata and simmer for another 5 minutes.
5. Grease a 9-inch tart pan. Unroll the pastry and press it into the pan. Prick the pastry bottom with a fork.
6. Spread the vegetable mixture into the tart pan and top with cheddar cheese.
7. Bake in the preheated oven for 25 minutes or until golden. Let cool for 10 minutes before slicing.

Nutrition information: Serving size (½ tart): Calories 250, Fat 17g, Saturated Fat 7.5g, Cholesterol 33mg, Sodium 298.4mg, Total Carbohydrates 17.4g, Sugars 5.7g, Protein 9g, Dietary Fiber 2.6g.

89. Soufflé au Grand Marnier

Soufflé au Grand Marnier is a decadent dessert featuring Grand Marnier liqueur, egg yolks, and sugar. This delicate mousse-like dessert is light and fluffy, and respects the flavour of the liqueur.
Serving - 6
Preparation time - 25 minutes
Ready time - 1 hour

Ingredients:
- 4 large egg whites
- 4 large egg yolks
- 1/2 cup sugar
- 1/2 teaspoon vanilla extract
- 1/4 cup all-purpose flour
- 1/4 teaspoon salt
- 2/3 cup hot milk
- 6 tablespoons Grand Marnier liqueur
- 4 tablespoons butter, melted and cooled
- Powdered sugar

Instructions:
1. In a large bowl, beat the egg whites with an electric mixer until peaks begin to form. Gradually add sugar and continue beating until stiff peaks form, about 4 minutes.
2. In a separate bowl, beat the egg yolks until pale yellow. Add vanilla extract and mix until combined.
3. Slowly sift in the flour and salt while continually mixing. Gradually pour the hot milk into the egg yolk mixture, stirring continuously.
4. Gently fold the egg white mixture into the egg yolk mixture until combined. Stir in the butter and Grand Marnier until evenly distributed.
5. Grease a 6-inch soufflé dish and pour the batter into the dish. Place the dish on a baking sheet and bake at 350°F for 40-45 minutes, or until the top is golden brown and the center is set.
6. Sprinkle with powdered sugar and serve.

Nutrition information - Calories: 427, Fat: 22g, Saturated Fat: 11g, Cholesterol: 172mg, Sodium: 281mg, Carbohydrates: 37g, Fiber: 0g, Sugar: 25g, Protein: 9g

90. Aligot

Aligot is a traditional French dish that combines mashed potatoes with a generous helping of melted cheese. This creamy, rich dish is incredibly easy to make and sure to please everyone.
Serving: 6
Preparation Time: 15 minutes
Ready Time: 45 minutes

Ingredients:
2 pounds potatoes
6 tablespoons butter
2 cloves garlic, minced
1/2 teaspoon salt, plus more to taste
1/2 teaspoon black pepper
1/4 teaspoon nutmeg
2–4 cups melted cheese (such as Gruyere, Comte, or Cantal)

Instructions:
1. Preheat oven to 350 degrees F.
2. Peel and cube potatoes and place in a large pot. Cover with cold water, bring to a boil, and cook for 20–25 minutes or until fork-tender.
3. Drain the potatoes and return to the pot. Add butter, garlic, salt, pepper, and nutmeg. Mash until creamy and smooth.
4. Transfer the potatoes to a large baking dish and spread evenly. Top with melted cheese.
5. Bake for 20–25 minutes or until cheese is bubbly and golden.
6. Serve hot.

Nutrition information: Serving size: 1/6 of the recipe; Calories: 288; Fat: 17.8 g; Cholesterol: 53 mg; Sodium: 466 mg; Carbohydrates: 24.3 g; Protein: 11.3 g

91. Oeufs en Meurette

Oeufs en Meurette is a traditional French dish made from poached eggs in a red wine sauce. This dish is perfect for a comforting dinner and can be served as a main dish or side dish.
Serving: 4
Preparation time: 15 minutes
Ready time: 35 minutes

Ingredients:
- 4 eggs
- 2 tablespoons butter
- 2 tablespoons all-purpose flour
- 2 cups dry red wine
- 2 cups beef stock
- 1 tablespoon tomato paste
- 2 cloves garlic, minced
- 1 teaspoon fresh thyme leaves
- 2 tablespoons chopped fresh parsley
- Salt and freshly ground black pepper

Instructions:
1. Heat the butter in a medium saucepan over medium-high heat.
2. Whisk in the flour until lightly browned, about 1 minute.
3. Whisk in the wine, beef stock, tomato paste, garlic, and thyme until combined.
4. Bring the mixture to a boil then reduce the heat and simmer for 10 minutes or until thick enough to coat the spoon.
5. Add the parsley and season with salt and pepper to taste.
6. Reduce the heat and crack the eggs into the sauce, one at a time.
7. Simmer for 5 minutes or until the eggs are cooked through.
8. Serve hot with crusty bread.

Nutrition information: Per serving: 426 calories, 24g fat, 28g carbohydrates, 14g protein.

92. Escargots à la Crème d'Ail

Escargots à la Crème d'Ail is a classic French dish consisting of snails cooked in garlic-infused cream.
Serving: 4

Preparation time: 20 minutes
Ready time: 55 minutes

Ingredients:
1 garlic bulb, cloves separated
2 tablespoons butter
3 tablespoons dry white wine
7 ounces canned escargots, drained
2 tablespoons chopped parsley
2 tablespoons heavy cream
Salt and freshly ground pepper, to taste

Instructions:
1. Preheat oven to 375°F. Peel the cloves from the garlic bulb and mince them.
2. In a medium skillet, melt the butter over medium heat and sauté the garlic cloves for 2 minutes.
3. Add the wine and escargots to the pan and sauté for 3 minutes. Add the parsley and cream and season with salt and pepper to taste.
4. Transfer the mixture to an oven-proof dish and bake for 30 minutes.

Nutrition information (per serving):
Calories: 182
Fat: 12g
Carbohydrates: 3g
Protein: 10g
Sodium: 442mg
Cholesterol: 34mg

93. Hachis Parmentier

Hachis Parmentier is a delicious French dish made with mashed potatoes, ground beef and cheese, topped with a crunchy layer of fried onions.
Serving: 4
Preparation time: 15 minutes
Ready time: 25 minutes

Ingredients:
- 4 large potatoes
- 1 lb ground beef
- 1 small onion, finely chopped
- 2 cloves of garlic, finely chopped
- ½ tsp ground nutmeg
- 1 tsp mixed herbs
- ¾ cup grated cheese
- 2-3 tablespoons olive oil
- Salt and freshly ground pepper to taste

Instructions:
1. Preheat the oven to 350°F (175°C).
2. Peel the potatoes and cut into 1-inch cubes. Place in a large saucepan with enough cold water to cover and season with salt. Bring to a boil and cook, uncovered, until tender, about 10-15 minutes. Drain and mash until smooth.
3. Heat the olive oil in a skillet over a medium-high heat. Add the ground beef and cook until browned, about 5 minutes. Add the onion and garlic and cook for an additional 3 minutes.
4. Add the nutmeg, herbs, salt, and pepper, and mix to combine. Cook for an additional 2 minutes.
5. Spread the mashed potatoes into a 9-inch baking dish and top with the ground beef mixture. Sprinkle the cheese over the top.
6. Heat a large skillet over medium-high heat and add the oil. Add the fried onions and cook until golden brown.
7. Top the casserole with the fried onions and bake in the oven for 10 minutes, until golden and bubbly.

Nutrition information:
Calories: 428, Protein: 20g, Total Carbohydrates: 38g, Dietary Fiber: 5g, Total Fat: 23g, Saturated Fat: 12g, Monounsaturated Fat: 3g, Cholesterol: 90mg, Sodium: 197mg, Potassium: 1168mg

94. Coquilles Saint-Jacques à la Provençale

Coquilles Saint-Jacques à la Provençale is a classic French dish made of stuffed scallops. It is a rich and flavorful dish that is perfect for special occasions.

Serving: 4
Preparation Time: 15 minutes
Ready Time: 50 minutes

Ingredients:
-8 Large Scallops
-4 strips of bacon
-1/4 cup of butter
-2 cloves of garlic
-1/2 cup of white wine
-2 shallots
-2 tablespoons of tomato paste
-1/2 cup of heavy cream
-1 tablespoon of fresh parsley
-2 tablespoons of grated Parmesan cheese

Instructions:
1. Preheat the oven to 375F.
2. Slice the bacon into small pieces.
3. Melt the butter in a skillet over medium heat and add the bacon. Cook for 3-4 minutes, or until the bacon is crispy.
4. Mince the garlic and add it to the skillet. Cook for a further 2 minutes.
5. Add the white wine and shallots, and cook until the liquid is reduced by half.
6. Stir in the tomato paste and heavy cream. Simmer for 2 minutes.
7. Place the scallops in an oven-proof dish, and pour the cream mixture over them.
8. Sprinkle with parsley and Parmesan cheese.
9. Bake for 20 minutes, or until the scallops are cooked.

Nutrition information: Per serving: 380 calories, 20g fat, 16g carbohydrates, 7g protein.

95. Navarin de Légumes

Navarin de Légumes is a French dish which traditionally uses mutton or lamb cooked Ingredients such as potatoes, carrots, onions and peas.
Serving: 4
Preparation Time: 10 minutes

Ready Time: 35 minutes

Ingredients:
- 2 tablespoons olive oil
- 2 cloves of garlic, crushed
- 2 diced onions
- 2 diced carrots
- 2 diced potatoes
- 2 diced turnips
- 300g lamb or mutton
- 1 teaspoon chopped fresh thyme
- 2 cups vegetable broth or water
- 1 tablespoon tomato paste
- 1 cup frozen peas
- Salt and pepper to taste

Instructions:
1. Heat the olive oil in a Dutch oven or other heavy pot over medium heat.
2. Add the garlic, onions, carrots, potatoes, and turnips and cook until the vegetables are lightly browned.
3. Add the lamb or mutton, thyme, broth or water, and tomato paste. Stir to combine.
4. Cover the pot and reduce the heat to low. Simmer for 20 minutes.
5. Add the frozen peas and season with salt and pepper. Simmer for an additional 15 minutes or until the vegetables are tender.
6. Serve hot with your favorite accompaniments.

Nutrition information:
Calories: 230 kcal; Fat: 7g; Carbs: 20g; Protein: 10g

96. Feuilleté de Camembert

Feuilleté de Camembert is a simple and delicious French pastry made with puff pastry and Camembert cheese. It is a great appetizer for entertaining and also makes a fantastic lunch or snack.
Serving: 4-6
Preparation Time: 15 minutes
Ready Time: 40 minutes

Ingredients:
- 1 sheet of frozen puff pastry, thawed
- 1 Camembert cheese
- 2 tablespoons of butter
- 2 tablespoons of fresh parsley, finely chopped
- 2 tablespoons of fresh chives, finely chopped
- 2 tablespoons of olive oil
- Salt and pepper to taste

Instructions:
1. Preheat oven to 350°F. Line a baking sheet with parchment paper.
2. Cut the puff pastry sheet into 4-6 equal rectangles. Place the rectangles on the baking sheet.
3. Place the Camembert cheese in the center of each rectangle. Slice the butter into small cubes and place the cubes on top of the cheese.
4. Sprinkle the parsley and chives over the cheese and butter. Drizzle the olive oil over the top.
5. Bake for 25-30 minutes until golden brown and bubbly. Season with salt and pepper to taste.

Nutrition information:
Calories: 300, Fat: 20 g, Carbohydrates: 19 g, Protein: 9 g, Sodium: 230 mg, Cholesterol: 15 mg

97. Croque Madame

Croque Madame is a delicious French dish that layers ham, cheese, and a creamy béchamel sauce between slices of buttered, toasted bread. It is often topped with a fried egg for a decadent finish.
Serving: 4
Preparation time: 10 minutes
Ready time: 25 minutes

Ingredients:
- 4 tablespoons butter, divided
- 8 thick slices of sturdy white bread
- 8 slices of ham

- 8 slices of Gruyère cheese
- 2 large eggs
- 3 tablespoons all-purpose flour
- 2 cups whole milk
- 2 tablespoons Dijon mustard
- Salt and pepper, to taste

Instructions:
1. Preheat the oven to 350°F.
2. Spread one tablespoon of butter on one side of each slice of bread. Place four of the buttered slices on a baking sheet and bake for 5 minutes.
3. Meanwhile, melt the remaining butter in a small saucepan over medium heat, then add the flour and form a paste. Cook the paste for two minutes, whisking constantly, then gradually add the milk, whisking until the sauce is smooth.
4. Bring the sauce to a light boil, then reduce the heat to low and add the mustard and a pinch of salt and pepper. Cook until the sauce is thickened, about 6 minutes.
5. Remove the sheet of toast from the oven and assemble the croque madame: Set a slice of ham on each piece of toast, top with a slice of cheese, then top with the remaining slices of toast, butter side out.
6. Return to the baking sheet and bake for an additional 10 minutes, until the cheese is melted and bubbly.
7. Meanwhile, fry or poach the eggs.
8. When ready to serve, place the croque madames on plates and top each one with a fried egg. Serve with additional salt and pepper, if desired.

Nutrition information: Per Serving: 350 calories, 22g fat (13g saturated fat), 135mg cholesterol, 737mg sodium, 20g carbohydrate (2g dietary fiber, 4g sugar), 17g protein.

98. Quiche au Saumon

Quiche au Saumon is a delicious French dish of pastry pie filled with salmon. It can be eaten as an appetizer or main course, and is sure to be a hit amongst family and friends.

Serving: 8
Preparation Time: 15 minutes
Ready Time: 45 minutes

Ingredients:
2 sheets of puff pastry
150 g of smoked salmon, cut into small cubes
2 eggs
120 ml of whole cream
25 g of grated cheese
Salt and pepper to taste

Instructions:
1. Preheat the oven to 180°C.
2. Place the puff pastry in a greased pie dish and trim off any excess.
3. Place the smoked salmon cubes in the pastry dish.
4. In a bowl, whisk together the eggs and cream until combined.
5. Pour the egg mixture over the salmon cubes and top with grated cheese.
6. Bake for 25 minutes or until the pastry has risen and is golden brown.
7. Let cool before serving.

Nutrition information: (Per Serving)
Calories: 290
Fat: 18.2g
Carbohydrates: 17.8g
Protein: 8.3g

99. Mille-Feuille

Mille-Feuille, also known as Napoleon, is a classic French pastry consisting of flaky pastry layers, vanilla-scented custard filling, and a thin powdered sugar glaze. This delicious dessert is sure to please all.
Serving: 12
Preparation Time: 2 hours
Ready Time: 4 hours

Ingredients:

- 2 boxes frozen puff pastry
- 6 cups heavy cream
- 3/4 cup granulated sugar
- 4 tablespoons cornstarch
- 2 tablespoons pure vanilla extract
- 2 sticks unsalted butter, room temperature
- Powdered sugar for dusting

Instructions:
1. Preheat oven to 375°F. Place a baking sheet in oven.
2. Place puff pastry on floured work surface. Cut each sheet into 4 by 4-inch squares. Place squares on preheated pan and bake for 18 to 20 minutes or until golden brown. Remove and let cool.
3. To make the custard, in a medium saucepan, bring cream to a boil. Add sugar, cornstarch, and vanilla extract, and whisk until smooth. Reduce heat snd simmer 3 to 5 minutes, stirring constantly until thickened. Remove from heat.
4. To assemble mille-feuille, arrange 12 puff pastry squares on serving dish. Spread 1/4 cup of custard onto each square. Top with another square of puff pastry. Spread butter over top and sprinkle with powdered sugar. Refrigerate for at least 2 hours.

Nutrition information: Per serving (1 mille feuille): 748 calories, 51g fat, 32g saturated fat, 162mg cholesterol, 352mg sodium, 57g carbohydrate, 1g fiber, 20g sugar, 10g protein.

100. Ficelle Picarde

Ficelle Picarde is a French dish made of thin and long slices of chewy baguette dough wrapped around a savory filling and fried until golden brown. It is served as an appetizer or a main course.
Serving: 4
Preparation Time: 10 minutes
Ready Time: 15 minutes

Ingredients:
• 4 pieces of baguette dough (ficelle)
• 1/2 cup of cooked ham or bacon, cut into strips

- 1/2 cup of shredded cheese
- 1/4 cup of onion, sliced
- 2 eggs
- 1 tablespoon of oil
- Salt and pepper, to taste

Instructions:
1. Preheat the oven to 375°F.
2. Slice the baguette dough into thin and long slices.
3. Grease a baking sheet with the oil.
4. Place the strips of baguette dough onto the baking sheet and top each one with the cooked ham or bacon strips, shredded cheese, and sliced onion.
5. Beat the eggs and pour over the slices of ficelle picarde.
6. Bake in the oven for 15 minutes until golden brown.
7. Remove from the oven and serve while still hot.

Nutrition information(per serving): Calories: 515; Fat: 23g; Carbohydrates: 51g; Protein: 23g; Sodium: 864mg; Sugar: 8g; Cholesterol: 98mg

101. Gratin de Chou-Fleur

Gratin de Chou-Fleur is an easy French dish prepared with cauliflower and cheese sauce, and topped with crunchy crumbs. It is a perfect side dish, but can also be enjoyed as a light lunch.
Serving: 4
Preparation time: 15 minutes
Ready time: 40 minutes

Ingredients:
- 1 head of cauliflower (about 2 pounds), cored and cut into florets
- 2 tablespoons butter
- 1 onion, finely diced
- 2 tablespoons all-purpose flour
- 2 cups whole milk
- 1 cup shredded Gruyère or other cheese of your choice
- ½ teaspoon sea salt

- Freshly ground pepper
- ½ cup plain bread crumbs

Instructions:
1. Preheat oven to 375 degrees Fahrenheit.
2. Place the cauliflower florets in a large pot and cover with water. Bring to a boil and cook until tender, about 8-10 minutes. Drain and set aside.
3. Melt the butter in a large saucepan over medium heat. Add the onion and cook until soft, about 3 minutes. Stir in the flour and cook for 1 minute. Gradually whisk in the milk and bring to a boil. Reduce the heat to low and simmer for 10 minutes, stirring occasionally. Remove from heat and stir in the cheese, salt, and pepper.
4. Spread the cauliflower in an oven-safe baking dish. Pour the cheese sauce over the top and sprinkle with the bread crumbs.
5. Bake in preheated oven for 20 minutes, or until golden brown and bubbly.

Nutrition information: Calories: 227, Total Fat: 10.5g, Saturated Fat: 6.3g, Trans Fat: 0g, Cholesterol: 36mg, Sodium: 500mg, Carbohydrates: 20.3g, Fiber: 4.2g, Sugars: 9.5g, Protein: 12.9g

102. Tarte au Fromage de Chèvre

Tarte au Fromage de Chèvre is a creamy goat cheese tart that has the perfect balance between sweet and savory flavors. It is a delightful dish that is perfect for any occasion.
Serving: 8-10
Preparation time: 15 minutes
Ready time: 1 hour

Ingredients:
- 2 roller sheets of puff pastry
- 200 g goat cheese
- 2 eggs
- 100ml cream
- 2 big onions
- 2 tablespoons olive oil
- Fresh thyme
- Salt and pepper

Instructions:
1. Preheat the oven to 180°C.
2. Thinly slice the onions and cut the puff pastry into circles to fit a nonstick tart pan.
3. In a skillet, heat 2 tablespoons of olive oil and fry the onions until golden brown. Season with salt, pepper, and fresh thyme.
4. Mix the eggs with the cream and spread the mixture over the puff pastry base.
5. Sprinkle the goat cheese over the egg and cream mixture.
6. Top with the caramelized onions and place the tart in the preheated oven for 40 minutes or until golden brown.
7. Let it cool for 10 minutes before serving.

Nutrition information: Per serving: 294 calories, 20.1 g fat, 10.4 g carbs, 11.9 g protein

103. Soupe de Potiron

Soupe de Potiron is a comforting and flavorful French pumpkin soup, featuring a rich blend of flavors enhanced by Herbs de Provence and crème fraîche. Slightly sweet and savory, this is a perfect one-pot meal that is sure to please!
Serving: This recipe serves 4 people.
Preparation time: 20 minutes
Ready time: 30 minutes

Ingredients:
• 4 cups chicken broth
• 2 cups diced pumpkin
• 4 tablespoons Herbs de Provence
• 2 tablespoons olive oil
• 2 cloves garlic, minced
• 1 onion, diced
• 1 teaspoon sea salt
• 1 teaspoon fresh ground black pepper
• 1 cup crème fraîche

Instructions:
1. Heat the olive oil in a large pot or Dutch oven over medium heat. Add the diced onion and garlic and cook until they begin to soften.
2. Add the diced pumpkin, broth, Herbs de Provence, sea salt and black pepper. Increase the heat to high and bring to a boil.
3. Reduce the heat to low and simmer for 25 minutes, stirring occasionally.
4. Remove from heat and let cool slightly. Using an immersion blender, blend the soup until creamy.
5. Return the soup to the pot and stir in the crème fraîche.
6. Serve hot.

Nutrition information
• Calories: 189 per Serving: • Fat: 11.5g per Serving: • Cholesterol: 20mg per Serving: • Sodium: 202mg per Serving: • Carbohydrates: 11.6g per Serving: • Protein: 6.4g per serving

104. Salade de Chèvre Chaud

Salade de Chèvre Chaud is a warm salad dish that combines fresh vegetables with warm toasted goat cheese. It is a great side dish for any meal, or can be served as a light lunch.
Serving: Serves 2
Preparation time: 10 minutes
Ready time: 15 minutes

Ingredients:
- 2 tablespoons of olive oil
- 2 cloves of garlic, minced
- 1 small red onion, diced
- 2 cups of mixed baby greens
- 2-3 tablespoons of balsamic vinegar
- 4 ounces of crumbled goat cheese
- Salt and pepper to taste

Instructions:
1. Heat olive oil in a large skillet over medium heat.
2. Add garlic and onion and cook for 3 minutes, stirring frequently.

3. Add the baby greens and cook for 2 minutes, stirring occasionally, until lightly wilted.
4. Add balsamic vinegar, goat cheese, salt and pepper to the pan and stir to combine.
5. Cook for an additional 2 minutes until the cheese is melted and slightly browned.
6. Divide the salad between two plates or bowls and serve.

Nutrition information: Calories: 320, Total fat: 23g, Saturated fat: 8g, Cholesterol: 25mg, Sodium: 415mg, Carbohydrates: 15g, Dietary fiber: 3g, Protein: 11g.

CONCLUSION

The cookbook Cocotte Cuisine: 104 Delicious Recipes has been a great reference for home cooks and professional chefs alike. From casual dinners to special occasions, the recipes featured in the book provide an array of creative, comforting, and easy-to-execute meals. The recipes range from classic French staples to universally loved dishes like beef bourguignon and creme brûlée. The cookbook also provides valuable tips alongside each recipe, from time and temperature guidelines to alternate methods depending on the desired doneness.

For home cooks, Cocotte Cuisine offers recipes for simple weeknight dinners as well as elaborately plated dishes for entertaining. Whether starting from a basic vinaigrette or learning how to make a signature roast chicken, the cookbook is an invaluable resource that showcases the versatility and depth of French cooking. Along with the recipes and techniques, the stories and photos shared throughout the book captivate the readers and make them feel like part of the culinary experience.

The cookbook not only educates readers about classic French cuisine, but also modern interpretations. As a guide to French cuisine, Cocotte Cuisine helps home cooks learn more about traditional and modern ingredients, techniques, and flavors. From recipes to garnish a steak to cooking an array of vegetables, the book helps cooks of any skill level find the perfect dish. Recipes can be adapted to accommodate a wide range of allergies, preferences, and dietary needs.

The cookbook serves as a wonderful reference point for cooks of all backgrounds and skill levels. Whether a beginner or veteran cook, the recipes, instruction, and tips can be tailored to suit the individual's needs. The flavorful recipes, stunning photos, and valuable knowledge contained within Cocotte Cuisine make it an exquisite guide to French cooking and cuisine.

Aradia
o il vangelo
delle Streghe

Charles G. Leland

2

İNTRODUZİONE

"Aradia, o il vangelo delle streghe d'italia" tradotto
dall'inglese "Aradia, or Gospel of witches" e
comunemente più noto come il "vangelo delle streghe",
rappresenta una delle pietre miliari a livello
internazionale, per quanto riguarda le tematiche legate al
fenomeno del neopaganesimo, ai diversi movimenti
Wicca e in generale a tutto l'ambiente legato
all'occultismo e all'esoterismo.

Il libro pubblicato in origine dall'autore Charles Godfrey
Leland, viene presentato come un antico manoscritto,
reperito dall'autore stesso durante i suoi viaggi
nell'entroterra tosco-emiliano, presentando l'opera come
un reperto di studio della tradizione popolare Italiana, un
sunto delle tradizioni mediterranee (Greco – Etrusche)
assimilate a tradizioni bibliche.

Leland introduce il manoscritto con un breve
commentario, dove espone le sue teorie storico
antropologiche sul folklore italiano, per poi procedere
rapidamente alla stesura del testo tradotto dall'italiano,
commentando saltuariamente alcuni passaggi. Nel suo
corpus l'insieme del manoscritto si presenta come un
"formulario" o "ricettario" di incanti e scongiuri sotto
forma di filastrocche, atti ad augurare la buona sorte o
scacciare il malocchio, purtuttavia non essendo mai
rinvenuto il testo originale e possedendo sole le

4